Who Is
Jesus?
Why Is He Important?

The **Come & See Series** from Sheed & Ward is modeled on Jesus' compassionate question: "What do you seek?" and his profound invitation to "Come and see" the world through the eyes of faith (John 1:38–39). The series offers spiritual seekers lively, thought-provoking, and accessible books that explore topics of faith and the Catholic Christian tradition. Each book in the series is written by trustworthy guides who are the very best teachers, theologians, and scholars.

Series Editors: James Martin, S.J.
Jeremy Langford

Who Is Jesus?

Why Is He Important?

An Invitation
to the
New Testament

Daniel J. Harrington, S.J.

SHEED & WARD
Franklin, Wisconsin

As an apostolate of the Priests of the Sacred Heart, a Catholic religious order, the mission of Sheed & Ward is to publish books of contemporary impact and enduring merit in Catholic Christian thought and action. The books published, however, reflect the opinions of their authors and are not meant to represent the official position of the Priests of the Sacred Heart.

1999

Sheed & Ward
7373 South Lovers Lane Road
Franklin, Wisconsin 53132
1-800-558-0580

Printed in the United States of America

Cover and interior design: Biner Design

Cover art used with permission of www.corbis.com/The
National Gallery, London
Scripture quotations are from the New Revised Standard Version of
the Bible, copyright 1989 by the Division of Christian Education of
the National Council of the Churches of Christ in the USA.
Used by permission. All rights reserved.

Library of Congress Cataloging-in-Publication Data
Harrington, Daniel J.
      Who is Jesus? why is he important?: an invitation to the New
   Testament / Daniel J. Harrington.
          p. cm. — (Come & See) .
      ISBN 1-58051-053-1 (pbk.)
      1. Jesus Christ—Person and offices—Biblical teaching. 2. Bible
   N.T.—Theology. I. Title II. Series.
   BT202.H294   1999
   232—dc21   98-49781
                                                        CIP

1 2 3 4 5 / 02 01 00 99

Contents

Preface

The New Testament is a book about Jesus of Nazareth. Or to state it more accurately, it is a collection of twenty-seven writings about Jesus. What joins together these writings is their focus on the person of Jesus and his significance. They all answer in somewhat different ways two basic questions: *Who is Jesus? Why is he important?* These writings were composed in Greek between the middle of the first century and the early years of the second century A.D. Almost two thousand years later, they are still being read in many languages by people all over the world. Some people regard them as classics or best-sellers. Others go further and call them Holy Scripture or the word of God.

This book is a beginner's guide to the writings of the New Testament. It is intended as a supplement to the primary sources, not a substitute for them. It leads the reader through the books of the New Testament by focusing on two questions that occupy most of their content: Who is Jesus? Why is he important? The first question concerns the identity of Jesus of Nazareth not only as a figure from the past but also as the risen Christ believed to be living now with his heavenly Father. The second question concerns the significance of Jesus for Christian life—for spirituality (how we stand before God and relate to others in light of this relationship), ethics (how and why we act), and the church (living alongside others who share faith in Jesus).

The introductory chapter supplies information about the content of the New Testament, sketches the historical setting when Jesus lived and when the early church developed, provides basic information about Jesus as a historical figure, and offers suggestions about how to read the New Testament. The nine chapters that follow treat the individual writings of the New Testament under headings that express their distinctive approach to Jesus and his significance. In each case there is a brief introduction that provides essential information about the book by answering some basic questions: Who? When? Where? Why? What? How? Next is an exposition of the major parts of the book, with an eye always to our two basic questions: Who is Jesus? Why is he important? Each exposition ends with some questions for reflection, discussion, meditation, or prayer. Since this book is an invitation, I have included a basic bibliography that can help the reader advance to the next stage in studying the New Testament.

Chapter 1

Books about Jesus

The first four books in the New Testament are called Gospels. They are narratives chiefly about Jesus' public ministry of teaching and healing and about his final suffering, death, and resurrection. The first three Gospels—Matthew, Mark, and Luke—follow a similar outline and present a similar vision of Jesus. They are usually referred to as the Synoptic Gospels. John's Gospel has some connections with the first three Gospels but presents a somewhat different outline and a more "spiritual" vision of Jesus. Matthew and Luke provide stories about Jesus' birth and infancy, Mark begins with John the Baptist and Jesus' baptism, and John traces Jesus' origin to the time before the world's creation ("In the beginning was the Word,…" John 1:1).

The Acts of the Apostles is also a narrative. It traces the spread of the good news about Jesus ("the gospel") from the time after Jesus' resurrection to Paul's imprisonment in Rome in the late fifties of the first century A.D. Composed by the writer of Luke's Gospel as a second volume, Acts devotes most of its attention to the deeds and speeches of Peter and Paul.

Letters written by Paul or circulated under his name constitute a large part of the New Testament. The thirteen Pauline epistles are divided into two groups: the nine letters that address communities (Romans to 2 Thessalonians) and the four letters that address individuals (1 Timothy to Philemon). The letters in these two groups are arranged from longest to shortest.

The statement "Paul's letter to the Hebrews" is misleading because its language, style, and theology are so different from Paul's that it could not have been composed by him. Though it has some elements of a letter, it is better understood as a sermon or homily. And it was written to and for Christians (probably Jewish Christians), not Hebrews.

Next come seven more letters—the Catholic Epistles. Here the word *catholic* carries its root meaning of "universal" and "for all." These seven short books—James; 1 and 2 Peter; 1, 2, and 3 John; and Jude—are recognized now by all Christians and regarded as relevant for all.

The final book is the Revelation (or Apocalypse) of John. The author (probably not the apostle or the evangelist) tells about his visions of God, the risen Christ, and the future. He speaks as a prophet and uses the conventions of ancient letters (see chapters 2 and 3).

All these books were written between the early fifties of the first century (1 Thessalonians) and the late first or early second century (2 Peter). All were written in the Mediterranean world—Palestine, Syria, Asia Minor (modern Turkey), Greece, and Italy. All appear to have been composed in Greek, which became the major language of the Mediterranean world after Alexander the Great's conquest (late fourth century B.C.) and continued as such under the Roman empire.

The Greek language of the New Testament books reflects both the speech of the common people (Koine Greek) and the influence of the Greek translation of the Hebrew Old Testament (Septuagint). The earliest Greek manuscripts of the New Testament are from the second to the tenth centuries. These are written all in capital letters without punctuation and without divisions between words. The Greek texts were translated fairly soon into Syriac, Latin, Coptic, Ethiopic, Armenian, and other languages. The ancient Greek manuscripts and the versions in other languages serve as the basis for the editions on which modern translations are based.

The most famous English Bible translation is the King

James or Authorized Version of 1611. Noted for its accuracy and high level of English, the King James Version has exercised enormous influence on the history of English speech and literature. By the nineteenth century, however, the need for new translations became evident. One reason was that the English language had changed over the centuries, and new translations had to take account of that fact. Moreover, specialists in the Greek New Testament recognized that the Byzantine Greek manuscript tradition on which the King James version was based was inferior in quality to the so-called Alexandrian family of manuscripts.

Many good translations of the Bible are available today: the New Revised Standard Version, New International Version, the New American Bible, the New Jerusalem Bible, the Revised English Bible, and the Good News Bible/Today's English Version. These range, as they are listed here, from the literal (formal equivalence) to the relatively free (dynamic equivalence). All are accurate and readable, but they reflect different translation philosophies and speak to different audiences. The New American Bible and the New Jerusalem Bible were prepared under Catholic auspices but involved Protestant scholars in the work. The others originated under Protestant auspices, though some of them too enlisted Catholic scholars in the translation project. The biblical quotations in this book are taken from the New Revised Standard Version, because it is generally accurate, widely available, current in its language and scholarship, gender inclusive (on the human level), and ecumenical in its team of translators.

The text of the Bible was divided into chapters in the twelfth century and into verses in the fifteenth century. All the modern editions and translations follow the same basic system of numbering chapters and verses. Rather than having to quote a text in full, one can simply cite the book, chapter, and verse. For example, Luke 1:32 and 1 Peter 5:13. The assumption is that the reader has access to a complete Bible and can look up the full text when necessary.

The World of the New Testament

The central affirmation of Christian faith is that "the Word became flesh and lived among us" (John 1:14). Christianity is an incarnational religion. It proclaims that God became one of us in Jesus of Nazareth. All the New Testament writers bear witness to Jesus, the Word who became flesh. Jesus lived his earthly life in Palestine, a small country on the eastern shore of the Mediterranean Sea and part of the Roman empire. Since all the books of the New Testament were written in the Mediterranean world in the second half of the first century or early second century, it is fair to describe earliest Christianity as a Mediterranean phenomenon.

The land in which Jesus was born is called Palestine or Israel. This was the homeland of the Jewish people and of Jesus the Jew. However, we must not regard the Israel of Jesus' day as sealed off from the Roman empire and the larger Mediterranean world. From the time of Alexander the Great (the late fourth century B.C.) the people of Israel were influenced by Hellenism in economics, military strategy, language, culture, and religion. Even when Hellenism was resisted by the Maccabees and others in religious matters, its influence in other areas continued to increase. Moreover, many Jews left the land of Israel and settled throughout the Mediterranean world. The term *Diaspora,* from the Greek for "disperse" or "scatter," was applied to Jews living outside the land of Israel. There were probably several million Jews living in the Diaspora in Jesus' time.

Moreover, the land of Israel was seething with political conflict. Becoming part of Alexander's empire initiated a long history of foreign domination and influence. A great crisis occurred in about 167–164 B.C. when the Syrian king Antiochus IV Epiphanes, with the encouragement of some members of the Jewish community in Jerusalem, tried to assimilate the worship in the Jerusalem Temple to foreign patterns. For the Maccabee family and the circle from which the book of Daniel originated, the traditional Jewish religion became a rallying point and source of resistance. The Maccabean revolt issued in an independent Israel that was, however, increasingly dependent on Rome's protection.

When in 37 B.C. Herod the Great gained control of the land of Israel by marrying into the Maccabee family, he began a series of building projects, including a large-scale expansion of the Jerusalem Temple. With his death in 4 B.C. one of his sons, Herod Antipas, took control of Galilee and held on to it until after Jesus' death. Another son, Archaelaus, lost control of Judea in A.D. 6 and was replaced by a series of Roman prefects or governors, of which the most famous was Pontius Pilate (A.D. 26–36). The cycle of political oppression, resistance, and repression led to revolts in A.D. 66–73 and 132–135. These uprisings ended in defeat for the Jews of Palestine and the loss of their Holy City and Temple, first in A.D. 70 and then more definitively in A.D. 135.

When Jesus lived (approximately 6 B.C. to A.D. 30), the center of Jewish religious and national life was the Jerusalem Temple. There was at the same time a current of dissatisfaction with and even opposition to the Temple among some in Jesus' home area of Galilee. Jews of Jesus' time were united by their belief in one God, their conviction that this God had entered into covenant with them and expected them to respond in certain ways (the Law or Torah), and that God had given the land of Israel to Abraham and his descendants.

Despite the obvious points of unity among Jews, there was much diversity within Judaism. Indeed, there were various ways of being a religious Jew. One could be a Pharisee, a Sadduccee, an Essene, a Zealot, a Samaritan, or a Christian, and probably many other things besides.

As Christianity moved out of the land of Israel, it spread chiefly through the cities of the Mediterranean world. The primary language in the Mediterranean cities was Greek, though Jews used Hebrew and Aramaic among themselves and Romans used Latin. By facilitating relatively safe travel by land and sea, the Roman empire contributed greatly to the spread of Christianity. Moreover, the *Pax Romana* ("Roman peace") encouraged people to move around the Mediterranean world as Paul and other missionaries did.

The chief cities of the Roman empire—Rome, Antioch, and Alexandria—had large Jewish populations. Early Christianity spread mainly through the efforts of Jewish Christians like Paul who used the local Jewish community as a base or at least an entry point. These Jewish communities attracted non-Jews who learned much about Judaism and its Scriptures. Such persons, known as "God-fearers," may have become the first Gentile Christians. Besides the synagogue, two other urban institutions that helped Christianity to grow were the household and the workplace. The early Christians met in large houses owned by wealthy members, and their number included less prosperous men, women, and even slaves. The workplace (for leather workers like Paul) provided the opportunity to meet new people and to share philosophies and religious doctrines.

People of the first-century Mediterranean region did not necessarily view the world and human relations in exactly the same way as we do. Whereas we exalt the importance of the individual, they defined themselves vis-à-vis their family, group, or tribe. To be admired and respected by others was honor, and to lose face before others was shame; both were pivotal values in Jesus' time. Whereas we proclaim that all persons are created equal, they assumed that some persons were born to rule and others were born to serve or to be slaves. To make one's way in the world one needed a patron or "godfather." Whereas we proclaim the separation of church and state, they found it difficult to distinguish between them because religious and political concerns were all mixed in together. Whereas we seek to expand the middle class and make it the center of democratic society, they assumed that most people (90 percent) would live on a subsistence income as peasants or artisans and that the ruling elite and their intermediaries would direct and profit from the rest of society. As we will see, the New Testament writers sometimes accepted the cultural values of their contemporaries (for example, Paul on slavery) and sometimes challenged them (John in Revelation on not participating in Roman civic religion).

Jesus of Nazareth

The four Gospels do not allow us to write a complete biography of Jesus or even a full account of his public ministry. One obvious problem is chronology. The Synoptic Gospels present Jesus' public activity in one year and with one journey to Jerusalem, whereas John spreads Jesus' activity over three years and recounts several journeys to Jerusalem. On the historical level, John's chronological framework is more likely. Another problem is that these writers never intended to write biographies of Jesus. Rather, they were trying to bring together traditions about Jesus and to present them in ways that would best highlight their beliefs in him as the risen Christ and the Son of God.

Nevertheless, the Gospels do allow us to discern a general outline of Jesus' life and to recognize the teachings that were most important to him. Jesus was born before the time of Herod the Great's death (4 B.C.) and was reared in Nazareth of Galilee. He was mentored and baptized by John the Baptist, but then embarked on his own ministry. He gathered disciples in his home area of Galilee. He proclaimed the coming kingdom of God and healed sick people in Galilee and (to a lesser extent) in Judea. He went up to Jerusalem for the last time in about A.D. 30 and was put to death by crucifixion under the Roman prefect or governor, Pontius Pilate. And he was said to have appeared alive again to many disciples.

The Gospels also allow us to reconstruct the major themes of Jesus' teaching. Jesus proclaimed the kingdom or sovereignty of God over all creation. For him, as for his Jewish contemporaries, the fullness of God's kingdom was in the future ("thy kingdom come"). But there were already anticipations or previews of it in the present. Jesus enjoyed a relationship of special intimacy with God as "Father" and invited his followers into that same relationship. He revealed to sinners the possibility of the forgiveness of sins and of reconciliation with God. He taught people how to act properly in anticipation of the coming kingdom of God. He challenged them to love all, even and especially their enemies. He showed a particular concern for marginal people—the economic poor, tax collectors (who were suspected of dishonesty and treason), sinners (who were unable or unwilling to observe the Jewish Law), and those suffering from sickness or other impairments (which were regarded as caused by sin). And he subordinated the Law and the Jerusalem Temple to the kingdom of God and took a free attitude toward the traditions and interpretations surrounding them.

Jesus' life ended suddenly and cruelly by crucifixion in A.D. 30. The ultimate legal responsibility lay with Pontius Pilate, the Roman prefect. According to the Gospels, the Jewish religious and political leaders encouraged or even forced Pilate to have Jesus executed. Jesus was perceived as a threat by both the Jewish leaders and the Roman officials, most likely because of his proclamation of the kingdom of God. To them he was another Jewish messianic pretender who was stirring up the Jewish people to revolt against the Roman authorities and their Jewish collaborators.

The official charge against Jesus involved the title "King of the Jews." To Pilate that title meant "messianic revolutionary." To the Jewish leaders it was the misuse of an expression with deep roots in Israel's history all the way back to David and Solomon. To early Christians, however, it spoke the truth about Jesus, the Messiah of Israel and the Savior of the world. One element in the development of this charge seems to have been Jesus' Temple action (see Mark 11:15–17; John 2:14–16) and his threat that the Jerusalem Temple would be destroyed and rebuilt by God (see Mark 14:58). Another element must have been the popular ferment aroused by Jesus' miracles and teachings and by the speculations about his identity as the Messiah (Mark 14:61–62). In some circles the Messiah was expected to drive out Israel's enemies and establish his rule over God's people. The Romans, of course, would have regarded anyone being called Messiah as a threat to their own rule. Likewise, their Jewish collaborators would have viewed Jesus as another threat to the peace and security of their people (see John 11:45–53).

There were in Israel other wise teachers, powerful healers, and Messiah-figures at this time. What made Jesus different?

What made him so important? All the New Testament writers try to answer these questions. They try to explain what made Jesus so different that he could be called the Son of God and Lord, that his death—rather than being a tragic mistake—was a necessary consequence of his life and teaching, and that it took place in accord with God's plan "for us" and "for our sins" in order to make possible a new relationship with God (justification and salvation).

How to Read the New Testament

The collection of twenty-seven writings that we call the New Testament, along with the books of the Old Testament, constitutes the "canon" of Christian Scripture. The word *canon* alludes to a measuring stick or ruler: the canon of Christian Scripture serves as the authoritative norm for measuring the church's faith and practice. All Christian churches today share the same twenty-seven book canon of New Testament writings.

For the early church and the New Testament writers, the canon of Scripture was the Old Testament. The New Testament canon developed only gradually. By A.D. 200 there was general agreement that the four Gospels, Acts, the thirteen Pauline letters, 1 John, and 1 Peter belonged in the Christian canon. There were disputes about accepting Hebrews, Revelation, and the other Catholic Epistles. By the late fourth and early fifth century, however, there was general agreement among the churches regarding the twenty-seven books that make up the canon of Christian Scripture.

As part of the canon, the books of the New Testament have a very high status among Christians. They are regarded as inspired by the Holy Spirit, as revealing what is necessary for salvation, and as containing the word of God in human words. They have a "divine" aspect. But there is also a "human" aspect, and so they demand a reading that attends to their literary, historical, and theological dimensions.

To begin to understand a New Testament book, we must read the text carefully and intelligently. A careful and intelligent reading of any text demands attention to its words and images, structure or progress of thought, literary form or genre, and content or message. These basic concerns of literary criticism are the necessary first steps in appreciating the beauty and depth of the New Testament writings.

The books of the New Testament originated in a specific place (the Mediterranean world) and time (the second half of the first century A.D.). Therefore they must also be read with the help of historical analysis. One of the historian's tasks is to trace the tradition behind a word or image, and here the Old Testament is a precious resource. Another historical task is to gather parallels from sources roughly contemporary with the New Testament. Such sources, whether they be Jewish or pagan, help us to understand what was "in the air," and what interpretations are possible or most plausible. The historian should also be something of a detective in trying to determine the sources behind a literary text and to reconstruct the actual events underlying the sources.

For most Christians, however, the New Testament is more than good literature or an interesting historical source. It is their primary source for Christian theology and Christian life. It raises and answers the two basic questions contained in this book's title: Who is Jesus? Why is he important? When we take these questions seriously, we engage in theological analysis. The New Testament writings deal for the most part with matters of theology and religious practice, and so they call for attention to matters of theology.

The nine chapters that follow focus on two questions: Who is Jesus? Why is he important? They deal with the twenty-seven books of the New Testament on three levels: literary, historical, and theological. Such a multilevel approach is entirely appropriate to these texts.

And yet it is not enough for most Christians to read carefully, to investigate historically, and to analyze theologically. They want to use the Sacred Scriptures in personal and communal prayer, Bible study groups, preaching, religious education, and other forms of "actualization." To actualize the Scriptures is to listen to their message, to let them speak to our lives in the present, and to face their challenges on both personal and communal levels.

This invitation to the New Testament paints in broad strokes. It intends to lead readers through the twenty-seven books by focusing on the person of Jesus and on what it means to follow him. It is written concisely and moves quickly through the various books. I recommend, however, that the reader pause along the way and reflect in some depth on the "Questions for Reflection" and on the specific passages listed in the "Texts for Special Attention" at the end of each chapter or each major section in those chapters that treat more than one book.

One ancient and effective way of reflecting and praying on Scripture is called *lectio divina* ("spiritual reading"). It proceeds in four steps. The first step is *reading:* determining what the text says by literary, historical, and theological analysis. The second step is *meditation:* exploring what this text says to me (or us) now. The third step is *prayer:* formulating what I (or we) want to say to God on the basis of this text. The fourth step can be *contemplation:* relishing and praising the ways of God; *action:* discerning what choices or changes God might be asking of me (or us) in light of this biblical text; or a combination of the two.

Using this reflective and prayerful method on specific texts along with the synthetic overview presented in the following chapters will help readers to enter into the central concerns of the New Testament and to accept its invitation to be with Jesus and to follow him.

Chapter 2

Teacher, Healer, and Suffering Messiah: Mark and Matthew

Popular culture has expressed enormous interest in Jesus recently. A few years ago three high circulation news magazines—*Time, Newsweek,* and *U.S. News & World Report*— had cover stories on "The Search for Jesus."

We have no books written by Jesus. What we do have and what must be the primary sources in "The Search for Jesus" are the four Gospels. The word *gospel* means "good news." In earliest Christianity the term referred to the saving significance of Jesus' death and resurrection. The earliest formulations of this gospel can be found in 1 Corinthians 15:3–5 and Romans 1:3–4.

The teachings of Jesus and accounts of his activities circulated in small units for about forty years after his death. The four large narratives in which these units now appear came to be called Gospels because they too proclaim the good news about Jesus' life, death, and resurrection. Now most people understand *gospel* to refer to a book about Jesus.

The writers of the Gospels are known as the Evangelists. The three Synoptic Gospels—Matthew, Mark, and Luke—share a similar outline of Jesus' public life and a similar vision of his significance. Most biblical scholars today regard Mark as the first Gospel, and Matthew and Luke as independent revisions and expansions of Mark. John's Gospel is quite different and represents an independent tradition about Jesus.

The four Evangelists present Jesus as a wise teacher and a model for Christian life. They wrote out of the conviction that Jesus was the most important person ever (because he is God's Son) and that, even though Jesus was put to death on the cross, he is still alive (because he was raised from the dead) and active in history through the Holy Spirit.

The Evangelists' portraits of Jesus, however, highlight different aspects of his identity and significance. This chapter and the two chapters that follow will focus on how each Evangelist answered in his own distinctive way the two basic questions that run through the entire New Testament: Who is Jesus? Why is he important?

Mark

The Christian literary category of Gospel seems to have been invented by the author known as Mark. Before his composition in about A.D. 70, the traditions about Jesus—his sayings and deeds—circulated in small units in both oral and written forms. Mark shaped these units into a connected narrative about Jesus' public ministry and about his passion and death. Early Christian tradition identified Mark as Peter's co-worker and interpreter. A setting in Rome seems likely, since the Evangelist presupposes an atmosphere of persecution and seeks to encourage a mainly Gentile Christian community (see Mark 7:3–4) to hold firm to its faith.

Mark presents the story of Jesus according to a geographical and theological outline. The first half takes place in Galilee: Jesus' authority as a teacher and healer is revealed in Galilee (1:1–3:6); Jesus is rejected in Galilee (3:7–6:6); and Jesus is misunderstood by his own disciples in Galilee and beyond (6:7–8:21). Then on the journey from Galilee to Jerusalem (8:22–10:45), Jesus instructs his disciples about who he is (Christology) and what it means to follow him (discipleship). The rest of the Gospel takes place in Jerusalem during passion week: three days of prophetic teachings and actions (11:1–13:37); and Jesus' Last Supper, arrest and trials, crucifixion and death, and the empty tomb (14:1–16:8).

Who is Jesus? According to Mark, Jesus is an authoritative teacher, a healer and miracle worker, and the suffering Messiah. Why is Jesus important? Because by his wisdom and example Jesus shows us a way of responding to God with courage and hope even in the midst of suffering and persecution.

Jesus is a teacher. The major theme of Jesus' teaching in Mark's Gospel is the kingdom of God. His first words provide an apt summary of his entire mission: "The time is fulfilled, and the kingdom of God has come near; repent and believe in the good news" (1:15). Jesus' public ministry represents the inauguration of God's reign among us in a new way. The proper response is to turn one's life around and believe in the good news (gospel) of the in-breaking of God's kingdom.

A teacher needs students. The story of the call of Jesus' first disciples (1:16–20) is peculiar. Here Jesus summons the disciples rather than having them come to him according to the usual Jewish custom. There is no indication that the first disciples knew Jesus beforehand. They were fishermen at the Sea of Galilee, with families and steady jobs. Yet when Jesus says "Follow me," they respond immediately and leave everything behind to become his disciples. How attractive and persuasive a teacher Jesus must have been to get this response!

The first large block of Jesus' teaching (2:1–3:6) takes the form of five controversies or debates. These debates concern the forgiveness of sins and healing on the Sabbath (2:1–12), eating with sinners (2:13–17), fasting and the compatibility of old and new (2:18–22), eating on the Sabbath (2:23–28), and healing on the Sabbath (3:1–6). In his debates Jesus confronts various opponents and shows his superior wisdom. His responses would have provided guidance for early Christian communities both in their practice and in their own debates within and outside the church.

Even though the kingdom of God is the center of Jesus' teaching, he never gives a precise definition of it. In fact, it is impossible to define something whose fullness is transcendent (it is God's kingdom) and future (it is God's to bring on "the day of the Lord"). And so Jesus the wise teacher uses parables—stories taken from nature or everyday life that are sufficiently mysterious so as to make people think more deeply and ask questions.

The most sustained sample of Jesus' teaching in Mark's Gospel consists of parables of the kingdom of God in 4:1–34. The seed parables (4:26–29, 30–32) go to the heart of the matter. They explicitly concern the kingdom: "The kingdom of God is as if . . ." The parable of the seed growing by itself tells us that something mysterious is happening in the present and that in God's good time the fullness of the harvest will come to pass. The parable of the mustard seed contrasts the small-ness of the present dimension of the kingdom (Jesus' ministry) and the great result that is coming forth in God's own time (the fullness of the kingdom). The parable about the seed and the sower and related material (4:3–25) explain that even though there is a mixed reception to Jesus' preaching of the kingdom, the harvest will be enormous where the seed meets good soil.

Mark's Jesus is also a healer and a miracle worker. The healings and other miraculous actions of Jesus are in the service of his central concern—God's kingdom. They illustrate how in Jesus' public ministry the power of God's kingdom is already manifest. The first miracle story—the healing of a man with "an unclean spirit" (a demon)—in 1:21–28 underlines the close relation between Jesus' teaching and his healing. It begins by describing the warm reception that Jesus' teaching got in the synagogue at Capernaum: "They were astounded at his teaching, for he taught them as one having authority, and not as their scribes." Next a man with an unclean spirit enters the synagogue, and Jesus exorcises the demon and restores the man to health. Then the crowd responds by linking the two aspects of Jesus' ministry: "A new teaching—with authority! He commands even the unclean spirits, and they obey him." His teaching and healing go together and confirm one another.

Large parts of Mark's Gospel are devoted to Jesus' acts of power—his healings, exorcisms, and nature miracles. One block of miracle stories appears in 4:35–5:43, immediately after the teaching in parables. In stilling the storm at sea (4:35–41), Jesus does what according to the Old Testament only God can do: He controls the chaotic forces of the sea. In freeing the Gerasene demoniac from his "legion" of demons (5:1–20), Jesus shows his power over Satan and the forces of evil. In restoring Jairus' daughter to life and healing the woman with the flow of blood (5:21–43), Jesus manifests his authority over chronic illness and even death.

These miracle stories make an important theological statement. Jesus is engaged in a battle with cosmic significance. He struggles against and overcomes the chaotic forces of nature, Satan, sickness, and death. In this respect his acts of power are part of his mission to proclaim and make present the kingdom of God. And so the disciples in 4:41 ask what is the central question in Mark's Gospel: "Who then is this, that even the wind and the sea obey him?"

Two components of the answer are clear already. Jesus is an authoritative teacher and a powerful miracle worker. But even more important for Mark is the recognition that Jesus is the suffering Messiah. The combination of those two words is hard to understand and still harder to accept.

Jesus' successes as a teacher and a miracle worker in the first half of Mark's Gospel are met by increasing hostility. First the Pharisees and Herodians conspire to destroy him (3:6). Then the people of his hometown take offense at him (6:3).

And finally even his own disciples fail miserably in understanding him (8:14–21).

The account of Jesus' journey to Jerusalem (8:22–10:52) clarifies who he is (the suffering Messiah) and what it means to follow him (take up the cross). His journey begins and ends with narratives (8:22–26; 10:46–52) in which a blind man comes to see; these stories are surely intended to describe more than physical sight. Along the way Jesus three times (8:31; 9:31; 10:33–34) predicts his passion, death, and resurrection. Knowing what awaits him in Jerusalem, Jesus moves forward with heroic courage. Yet at each point the disciples fail to understand him, which in turn provides an opportunity for further instruction on Christology and discipleship.

When Jesus reaches Jerusalem, there is at first a popular welcome (11:1–11). Then, however, there is increasing hostility exemplified by Jesus' prophetic actions against the corruption of the Temple establishment (11:12–25), his debates with various opponents (11:27–12:37), and his last discourse about the destruction of the Temple and the coming of the Son of Man in glory (13:1–37).

The plot to kill Jesus is initiated by one of his own disciples (Judas) in collaboration with the Temple officials and their supporters. Jesus is charged with plotting to destroy the Temple (14:48) and with claiming to be the Messiah (14:61).

The word *messiah* means "anointed." In ancient Israel it was customary to anoint priests, prophets, and kings. Some

Jews in Jesus' time hoped that God would send a Messiah—a powerful warrior and righteous king like David—who would restore Israel to religious, political, and economic greatness. To the Roman officials and their Jewish supporters, such talk about a Messiah was dangerous. And they moved quickly to put Jesus to death by crucifixion—a public punishment inflicted on rebels and slaves (15:21–41).

What Jesus' opponents and even his disciples could not understand is that Jesus was a different kind of Messiah. He was from the house of David. He was sent by God. He was the Messiah of Israel. But he was a suffering Messiah. His suffering was not only exemplary (he provided a good example for suffering people) but also efficacious (it really accomplished something): "For the Son of Man came not to be served but to serve, and to give his life as a ransom for many" (10:45). This Messiah was sent to conquer not the historic enemies of Israel but rather death itself through his resurrection. When his tomb was found empty on Easter Sunday, the correct interpretation was "he has been raised; he is not here" (16:6). In many New Testament writings (especially Romans, Hebrews, and Revelation) what is most important about Jesus is his death and resurrection "for us."

According to Mark, Jesus is a teacher, healer and miracle worker, and the suffering messiah. The disciples make a good beginning by answering Jesus' call and following him (1:16–20). They share his invitation to "be with him" (3:14) and his mission of healing and proclaiming God's kingdom (6:7–13). Yet as the narrative proceeds, these disciples become increasingly a negative example. They repeatedly fail to understand Jesus, and at the time of his arrest they abandon him. At the same time, we learn about a group of faithful women disciples. They stand by the cross of Jesus (15:40–41), see where he was buried (15:47), and find his tomb empty (16:1–8). Their fidelity contrasts with the infidelity of the first male disciples.

Jesus faces death as a hero. He accepts his fate as God's will, though not without some resistance (see 14:32–42). For Christians who suffer and especially those who undergo persecution for their faith, the Markan Jesus provides a model of fidelity to God. His public ministry and his saving death mark decisive steps in the coming of God's kingdom. But the full coming remains future (see Mark 13). Christian life, according to Mark, is lived under the shadow of the cross and against the horizon of God's kingdom. The proper attitude in the present is constant vigilance (see 14:32, 35). Formed by Jesus' teaching and example, Christians live in the hope that they will see "the Son of Man seated at the right hand of the Power" (14:62).

Questions for Reflection: *How would you describe the content of Jesus' teaching about God's kingdom according to Mark? What does it mean to follow Jesus? How might Mark's story of Jesus encourage suffering Christians?*

Texts for Special Attention: *Mark 1:14–20; 4:3–9; 4:35–41; 8:14–21; 9:2–8; 12:13–17; 14:3–9; 14:55–65; and 15:21–39.*

Matthew

Matthew's Gospel is a revised and expanded version of Mark. Tradition links the author to the tax collector named Matthew whom Jesus called to be an apostle (Matthew 9:9), though the actual composition of the Gospel was complex and extended over many years until around A.D. 85 or 90. The Evangelist whom we call Matthew wanted to supplement Mark's narrative with teaching materials and other traditions, most notably the infancy narratives. He also sought to speak to the situation of his largely Jewish Christian community after the destruction of the Jerusalem Temple in A.D. 70. Matthew's community lived in an eastern Mediterranean city where Greek was the main language and where there was a large Jewish community. Antioch in Syria is the most likely candidate for the Gospel's place of origin.

Matthew was responding to a crisis that faced all Jews in the late first century. Without the Temple and with even less direct control over the land of Israel, how could Judaism continue? Matthew's answer was that authentic Judaism is best carried on by those gathered around Jesus as Lord and Teacher. Other Jews had other answers: military rebellion (Zealots), careful observance of God's Law and gathering the traditions associated with Israel's teachers (the early rabbis), and waiting for God to intervene (apocalyptists).

In producing a revised and expanded version of Mark's Gospel, Matthew followed the basic outline of Jesus' ministry in Galilee, his journey up to Jerusalem, and his passion, death, and resurrection in Jerusalem. At the beginning (chaps. 1–2) Matthew presents material about Jesus' birth and infancy. At the end (28:9–20) he adds two resurrection appearances and a story about the empty tomb. Matthew's most obvious structural feature, however, lies in the alternation of five blocks of narrative (chaps. 3–4, 8–9, 11–12, 14–17, 19–23) and five speeches (chaps. 5–7, 10, 13, 18, 24–25).

Who is Jesus according to Matthew? Since Matthew is revising Mark, Jesus is a teacher, a healer and miracle worker, and the suffering Messiah. Matthew brings out some other dimensions of Jesus: He is the fulfillment of Israel's hopes, the only teacher, and the founder of the church. These emphases speak both to the historical situation of the Gospel's composition and to Christian people today.

Matthew's Jesus is the fulfillment of Israel's hopes. It is common to describe Matthew as the most Jewish Gospel. Matthew emphasizes Jesus' Old Testament and Jewish background, portrays Jesus and his disciples as within Judaism, and addresses a conflict between Christian Jews and other Jews in the late first century. Without the Old Testament and Judaism, Matthew's Gospel makes no sense.

The infancy narrative (chaps. 1–2) begins by rooting Jesus in the history of Israel: Jesus is the descendant of Abraham, David, and the exile generation (1:1–17). Through Joseph, Jesus is a legal descendant of King David (1:18–25). He is "Emmanuel"—a figure prophesied by Isaiah—bearing a name that means "God with us." The Gospel ends with the risen Jesus' promise to "be with you always" (28:20).

An important feature of Matthew's infancy narrative is the fulfillment of Scripture. At several points it is said that "all this took place to fulfill what had been spoken by the Lord through the prophet." The Scriptures represent God's promises to and will for Israel. At every step the prophecies are being carried out in the infancy of Jesus. The Scripture fulfillments are scattered through Matthew's account of Jesus' public ministry and reach a climax in the passion narrative (chaps. 26–27) where Jesus' suffering is interpreted with the help of the righteous sufferer of Psalm 22 and the suffering servant of Isaiah 53. For Matthew, Jesus is the key to the Old Testament Scriptures; in him they reach their fulfillment.

The Matthean Jesus is also the only teacher. That claim is made most explicitly in 23:10: "Nor are you to be called instructors, for you have one instructor, the Messiah." Matthew greatly expanded Mark by adding many teachings of Jesus. Even though Mark emphasized the authority of Jesus as a teacher, he gave only a relatively small sample of the content of his teaching. Matthew and Luke independently used a collection of Jesus' sayings (known among scholars as Q) and other traditions to flesh out the content of Jesus' teaching.

The most famous block of Jesus' teaching is the Sermon on the Mount (chaps. 5–7). The sermon first declares "blessed" or "happy" some surprising people: the poor in spirit, those who mourn, the meek, and so forth (5:3–12). Then it shows how on various topics in the Old Testament Law (murder, adultery, divorce, oaths, retaliation, enemies) Jesus goes to the root of the matter and yet manages to uphold the real intention of the Law ("not to abolish but to fulfill," 5:17). Then in 6:1–18 Jesus insists that the practices of piety—almsgiving, prayer, and fasting—should be done to please God rather than to gain a reputation for personal holiness. The Lord's Prayer (6:9–13) is an example of a short prayer for the coming of God's kingdom in its fullness ("Thy kingdom come"). The rest of the sermon (6:19–7:27) concerns various "deeds of loving-kindness." The best-known saying is the Golden Rule: "In everything do to others as you would have them do to you" (7:12).

The Sermon on the Mount is followed in chapters 8–9 by a block of nine (or ten) miracle stories interrupted twice by discipleship material. The point is that Jesus is powerful both in word (teacher) and in deed (miracle worker).

In two of the five great speeches—chapters 13 and 24–25—Matthew builds upon the discourses in Mark 4 and 13, respectively. In chapter 13 Matthew adds several parables that highlight both the present and the future dimensions of God's kingdom. And his eschatological discourse in chapters 24–25 includes many parables that contribute to the theme of the need for constant vigilance in Christian life, especially when the master's return seems to be delayed.

Matthew's Jesus is also the founder of the church. That does not mean that Jesus planned out all the structures and offices of the church. However, Matthew's Gospel does allow us to see in Jesus' teaching and activity some elements that have shaped the church and Christian life throughout its history.

The speech in chapter 10 is called the missionary discourse. Here Jesus sends out his disciples to continue his mission of preaching God's kingdom and healing the sick. He urges them to follow a simple lifestyle and to expect persecution, on the grounds that "a disciple is not above the teacher" (10:24). The fourth great speech (chap. 18) is aptly described as Matthew's advice to a divided community. In it Jesus deals with true greatness in the kingdom of heaven ("become like children"), temptations to sin, the problem of those who stray (the parable of the lost sheep), correcting a member who sins, and forgiveness within the community.

Peter is an important figure in Matthew's Gospel. As in Mark, Peter is one of the first disciples called by Jesus and often serves as the spokesman for the Twelve. There are, however, two important passages unique to Matthew's Gospel in which Peter plays a central role. In the story of Jesus walking on the water (14:22–33) Peter tries to do the same. He succeeds for a while. But when Peter begins to sink, he cries out "Lord, save me!" Peter appears as an example of "little faith," which is Matthew's characteristic way of describing Jesus' disciples who have some faith but not perfect faith.

Peter's confession of faith in Jesus (16:16–19) is among the most famous texts in the Bible. When Peter correctly identifies Jesus as "the Messiah, the Son of the living God," Jesus declares Peter blessed because God had revealed this to him. Jesus goes on to promise to build his church on Peter (whose name means "rock") and to stand behind Peter's decisions. According to Christian tradition, Peter eventually came to Rome, served as bishop there, and died a martyr's death. This passage has traditionally functioned as the biblical foundation for the papacy; that is, the bishop of Rome as the successor of Peter.

Matthew's Gospel ends (28:16–20) with the risen Jesus' commission to the eleven remaining disciples (minus Judas the betrayer) and by extension to the church throughout the centuries: "make disciples of all the nations, baptizing them . . .

and teaching them." This commission is rooted in the authority of Jesus and is guaranteed to have the help of the risen Jesus ("I am with you always, to the end of the age"). All these elements in Matthew's Gospel—the missionary discourse, the advice to the community, the prominence of Peter, and the great commission—contribute to the idea that Jesus is the founder of the church.

Matthew's emphases on Jesus as the fulfillment of Israel's hopes, as the only teacher, and as the founder of the church spoke to the historical setting in which his Gospel was composed. In the crisis that faced all Jews in the late first century, Matthew insisted that Jesus was the key to the Jewish Scriptures and that God's promises to Israel were being fulfilled in him. Over against Jews who were gathering the teachings of many rabbis, Matthew put forward Jesus as the only teacher and as the authoritative interpreter of Israel's religious tradition. As the new situation after the destruction of the Jerusalem Temple demanded new institutions and new forms of religious and community life, Matthew traced the mission and lifestyle of the church back to Jesus and his earliest disciples. The polemical language of chapter 23 ("woe to you, scribes and Pharisees, hypocrites!") reflects the seriousness of the struggle about how and where Israel's religious heritage was to be continued.

Why is the Matthean Jesus important today? Matthew places Jesus within Judaism as the fulfillment of God's promises to Israel, thus providing a constant reminder of the Jewish religious heritage of Christianity. We cannot understand Jesus without knowing and respecting the Scriptures of Israel. The large amount of Jesus' teachings that Matthew makes available to us supplies guidance for living the Christian life in the spirit of Jesus. The Matthean Jesus' teachings deal with love of God and neighbor; wealth and poverty; marriage and divorce; and many other perennially important topics. And these teachings are placed against the horizon of God's kingdom and in the context of discipleship.

With his interest in the church, Matthew reminds us that Christian life is always communal, that even in the early church there were conflicts and apostasies, and that the mission of the church is to continue the movement begun by Jesus. At the same time, what is said about the church in Matthew's Gospel can serve as a measure by which we can assess the fidelity of the church in every age.

Questions for Reflection: *Why is Matthew's Gospel considered the most Jewish? What teaching of Matthew's Jesus impresses you most? How might the advice in Matthew 10 and 18 help in dealing with problems in your church?*

Texts for Special Attention: *Matthew 1:18–25; 5:3–12; 6:1–18; 6:25–34; 10:5–15; 11:25–30; 13:44–50;*

14:22–33; 16:16–19; 18:21–35; 19:16–22; 27:33–54; and 28:16–20.

Chapter 3

Glory of Israel and Light to the Gentiles: Luke–Acts

Luke's Gospel and the Acts of the Apostles constitute a two-volume work. The Gospel tells the story of Jesus from his birth to his death and resurrection. Acts moves from the ascension of Jesus to Paul's imprisonment in Rome. The author of these two volumes has been traditionally identified as Luke, one of Paul's co-workers (see Col 4:14; Philem 24; 2 Tim 4:11). Though most likely a Gentile, Luke knew much about the Jewish Scriptures and Jewish customs. In the second half of Acts there are several passages where the narrator speaks in the first-person plural ("we") as if he had accompanied Paul on his journeys.

Even though his narrative breaks off in the early sixties

(before Paul's death), Luke most likely composed his work around A.D. 85 or 90. Some passages in the Gospel seem to refer to the destruction of Jerusalem in A.D. 70 (see Luke 19:43–44; 21:20, 24). Where the author wrote remains uncertain. Practically everywhere in the Mediterranean world—Rome, Greece, Asia Minor, Antioch in Syria, and Caesarea Maritima in Palestine—has been mentioned.

Luke's Gospel

In the preface to his Gospel (1:1–4), Luke tells about his methods and goals. He dedicates his work to Theophilus. The name means "lover of God," and whether it refers to a real person (a patron) or is a symbolic reader is hard to know. Luke proposes to present "an orderly account" so that Theophilus and other readers "may know the truth concerning the things about which you have been instructed"—about Jesus' birth, public ministry, passion and death, and resurrection. He acknowledges the work of his predecessors whom he calls "eyewitnesses and servants of the word."

Like Matthew's Gospel, Luke's Gospel is a revised and expanded edition of Mark's Gospel. Luke took over the basic narrative—ministry in Galilee, journey to Jerusalem, and passion and death in Jerusalem—and most of the content from Mark. As Matthew did about the same time, Luke included many teachings from the Sayings Source, and supplemented Mark and that source with other special traditions.

Luke set out to write an orderly narrative about the life, death, and resurrection of Jesus on the basis of traditional materials and so to inspire confidence in his readers about the foundations of their Christian faith. His story of Jesus can be divided into three major parts. The first part (1:5–4:13) concerns the birth of Jesus and the preparations for his public ministry. The second part (4:14–21:38) tells about Jesus' ministry in Galilee (4:14–9:50), his journey to Jerusalem (9:51–19:44), and his ministry in Jerusalem (19:45–21:38). The third part (22:1–24:53) deals with Jesus' passion, death, and resurrection in Jerusalem.

Who is Jesus for Luke? Jesus is the glory of Israel and a light to the Gentiles, a prophet, and a martyr. Jesus provides a good example in every facet of his life. He is a teacher who is completely faithful to his own teachings.

Luke's Jesus is the glory of Israel and the light to the Gentiles. That description echoes the words of Simeon's blessing upon the child Jesus in the Jerusalem Temple (2:32). These two themes dominate the first major part of Luke's Gospel (1:5–4:13) and run through the rest of the Gospel and through the whole of Acts. The story of Jesus begins in the Jerusalem

Temple—the most sacred place in Israel—with the promise of a child (John the Baptist) to Zechariah and Elizabeth. When the birth of Jesus is announced to Mary in Nazareth of Galilee, she is told that her child will be called "the Son of the Most High" and will "reign over the house of Jacob forever" (1:32–33). The two great hymns of Luke 1—Mary's song of praise and Zechariah's prophecy—celebrate the action of the God of Israel in the birth of Jesus. The child Jesus is born in Bethlehem, the ancestral home of King David. In the Jerusalem Temple, Simeon and Anna prophesy great things for him. At the age of twelve Jesus is found in the Temple ("my Father's house," 2:49) conversing with the great teachers. Everything in the infancy narrative (Luke 1–2) points to Jesus as the glory of Israel, and he is among persons who stand for all the best in the Jewish tradition.

Luke's Jesus is at the same time a light to the Gentiles. Luke places Jesus' birth in the context of a decree from the emperor (2:1–7). He describes Jesus in terms used elsewhere for Augustus in a Greek inscription ("savior . . . he will make wars cease . . . the birthday of this god . . . the gospel festivals"). In introducing the public activity of John the Baptist and Jesus, Luke in 3:1–2 carefully lists the names of the emperor (Tiberius), the governor (Pontius Pilate), and other officials, thus placing John and Jesus in the context of world history. In tracing the ancestors of Jesus (3:23–38), Luke moves the genealogy back through David and Abraham to Adam as the ancestor of all humans. All these texts indicate that Jesus has significance not only for Israel but also for all humankind (a light to the Gentiles).

This light to the Gentiles is the Son of God. At the baptism, the heavenly voice identifies Jesus as "my beloved Son" (3:21–22). The genealogy describes Adam as "son of God," suggesting that Jesus is the new Adam. The temptation narrative (4:1–13) shows what kind of Son of God Jesus is. When challenged by Satan to prove his divine sonship ("if you are the Son of God"), Jesus refuses to subordinate himself to Satan and manifests perfect fidelity to God as his Father. Then Satan leaves the scene (4:13), to return only at the beginning of the passion narrative (see 22:3).

Luke's account of Jesus' public ministry (4:14–21:38) focuses on Jesus as the prophet of God. In the Old Testament a prophet was called by God to speak God's will before the people. The prophet's message was often discomforting and accompanied by symbolic actions. Prophets were not always popular since they challenged the people to change their ways. In New Testament times there was speculation about the coming of a prophet like Moses (see Deut 18:15). In his public ministry, Jesus acted like a prophet by calling the people to repent, by using parables and symbolic actions as teaching tools, and by warning about the judgment that will accompany the fullness of God's kingdom.

The very first scene in Jesus' public ministry (4:16–30) identifies him as a prophet. His reading from Isaiah 61:1–2 sketches his own mission as God's prophet. He is the bearer of the Holy Spirit; he is to bring good news to the poor, to set people free, and to proclaim God's favor. In his one-sentence sermon (4:21) Jesus says: "Today this scripture has been fulfilled in your hearing." Jesus takes as his models the prophets Elijah and Elisha, two Israelite prophets who ministered to Gentiles. But the people of Nazareth apparently refused to accept that Jesus could be a light to the nations. Lack of popular acceptance is part of being a prophet, and so it is not surprising that the crowd's initial interest should turn to hostility, so that Jesus has to escape to save his life (4:28–30).

The preface to Jesus' public ministry in 4:16–30 places his entire ministry in Galilee (4:31–9:50) and beyond in a prophetic context. Like Elijah and Elisha, Jesus issues challenging teachings, performs healings and other miracles, and arouses opposition. In restoring to life the son of the widow of Nain (7:11–17), Jesus does what both Elijah (1 Kgs 17:17–24) and Elisha (2 Kgs 4:8–37) did before him. And so it is not surprising that the witnesses proclaim "a great prophet has arisen among us!" and "God has looked favorably upon his people." In the episode about the sinful woman (7:36–50), Jesus' Pharisee host grumbles: "If this man were a prophet, he would have known who and what kind of woman this is who is touching him—that she is sinner" (7:39). In fact, the story goes on to show that Jesus the prophet knows exactly what kind of woman she is and forgives her sins nonetheless.

The most distinctive structural feature in Luke's Gospel is its very long journey narrative. What Mark told in slightly more than two chapters (8:22–10:52), Luke expanded to more than ten chapters (9:51–19:44). He clearly used the journey as a vehicle for including more of Jesus' teachings. Many of the most famous and beloved passages in the Bible are included in Luke's journey narrative: the good Samaritan (10:25–37); Mary and Martha (10:38–42); the teachings on prayer (11:1–13); the banquet teachings (14:1–24); the parables of the lost sheep, the lost coin, and the lost son (15:1–32); the rich man and Lazarus (16:19–31); and the story of Zacchaeus (19:1–10).

The journey begins on an ominous note: "When the days drew near for him to be taken up, he set his face to go to Jerusalem" (9:51). This journey will end with Jesus being "taken up." The expression is a preview of Jesus' arrest, trial, death, resurrection, and ascension, as well as an allusion to the assumption of the prophet Elijah (see 2 Kgs 2:1–12). Though he knows his fate, Jesus the prophet nevertheless "set his face to go"—a phrase that indicates Jesus' free decision to accept God's will for him. The goal of the journey is Jerusalem, the place where prophets are rejected and even killed.

As the journey proceeds, we are reminded in 13:33–34

about the purpose of the journey: "Yet today, tomorrow, and the next day I must be on my way, because it is impossible for a prophet to be killed outside of Jerusalem." As the journey ends (19:41–44), Jesus the prophet weeps over Jerusalem because he foresees its destruction by the Romans: " … your enemies will set up ramparts around you, … they will crush you to the ground, … they will not leave within you one stone upon another."

Jesus' ministry in Jerusalem (19:45–21:38) begins with his prophetic action in the Temple (19:45–48). Using the words of the prophets Isaiah ("My house shall be a house of prayer," Isa 56:7) and Jeremiah ("a den of robbers," Jer 7:11), he takes possession of the Temple as "my house" (see "my Father's house," in 2:49). He teaches in the Temple area regularly (see 19:47; 20:1; 21:5–6, 37–38) and there delivers his prophecy about the destruction of the Temple ("not one stone will be left upon another") and the city of Jerusalem (21:20–24). When the risen Jesus encounters the disciples on their way to Emmaus, they describe Jesus as "a prophet mighty in deed and word before God and all the people" (24:19). Jesus' identity as a prophet is the thread that binds together Luke's account of his public ministry.

The Lukan Jesus is also a martyr in the root sense of faithful witness. In retelling the story of Jesus' passion and death (22:1–24:53), Luke presents Jesus as a good example and as willingly going to death out of fidelity to his Father's will and to his own teachings. At the Last Supper Jesus interprets his coming death as the service of others: "But I am among you as one who serves" (22:27). He is declared innocent in 23:1–12 by both the Roman governor (Pontius Pilate) and the ruler in Galilee (Herod Antipas). Nevertheless, Jesus is sentenced to death. He is clearly an innocent sufferer.

In his three last words from the cross, Jesus shows himself to be a faithful witness to his own teachings. In 23:34 he asks that his heavenly Father forgive those who put him to death, thus practicing his teaching about loving one's enemies. In 23:43 he continues his ministry to outcasts by promising the "good thief" a place in God's kingdom. In 23:46 his last words, which are taken from Psalm 31:5 ("Father, into your hands I commend my spirit"), illustrate perfectly his own teachings about trust in God. The innocent Jesus dies as a witness (the root meaning of *martyr*) to the cause of God.

Luke's Gospel has been described as the most beautiful book ever written. Its portrait of Jesus as the glory of Israel and the light to the Gentiles, as the prophet, and as the martyr has inspired and challenged people for centuries. Yet it is more than a beautiful story about someone who lived long ago and far away. Rather, it continues to challenge us to take seriously the reversal of values proclaimed in Mary's song ("he has filled the hungry with good things, and sent the rich away empty," 1:53) and the beatitudes ("Blessed are you poor," 6:20). Luke also promotes the life of prayer. His Jesus prays at all the important points of his life and provides ample teachings about prayer (see 11:1–13; 18:1–14). Luke highlights the role of women not only in the infancy narrative but also in the public ministry of Jesus (8:1–3). The true disciples of Jesus are "those who hear the word of God and do it" (8:21; see 11:28). According to this definition, Mary the mother of Jesus is the perfect disciple (see 1:38, 45; 2:19).

Questions for Reflection: *How does Luke portray Jesus as significant for both Jews and Gentiles? What is a prophet in the light of Jesus' identity as a prophet? Does Luke's presentation of Jesus' death help you to understand what a martyr is?*

Texts for Special Attention: *Luke 1:26–38; 1:46–55; 4:16–30; 6:20–49; 10:25–37; 11:1–13; 15:11–32; 16:19–31; 19:1–10; 22:14–30; 23:32–49; and 24:13–35.*

Acts

If Luke's Gospel is the most beautiful book ever written, his Acts of the Apostles surely qualifies as one of the great adventure stories. Acts is the account of how the gospel spread "in Jerusalem, in all Judea and Samaria, and to the ends of the earth" (Acts 1:8). It is the story of how the great apostles (especially Peter and Paul) carried on Jesus' mission and how the gospel came to the Gentiles under the guidance of the Holy Spirit.

Luke's second volume is also dedicated to Theophilus (1:1). As in his Gospel, Luke had access to and used earlier sources. The problem is that Luke has so skillfully integrated these sources that it is now hard to distinguish between what came from these sources and what Luke composed on his own. Even in the case of the "we" passages (see 16:11–12, 16, etc.) it is not clear whether Luke is relating his personal experiences, quoting from someone else's travel journal, or simply making his narrative more vivid.

After narrating the ascension of Jesus (1:1–11), Luke describes the growth of the church in Jerusalem (1:12–8:3), its expansion out to Judea and Samaria (8:4–9:31), the various missions to the Gentiles and to the Jerusalem council (9:32–15:35), Paul's second (15:36–18:23) and third (18:24–21:14) missionary journeys, his imprisonment and witness to Jesus

(21:15–26:32), and his voyage to Rome (27:1–28:31).

Acts is full of good historical information and good theology. Some interpreters take Acts as a historical guidebook, and others see it as a series of edifying vignettes. Acts, of course, is both history and theology. But first of all it is a story—a great adventure story that is told in a vivid and interesting style. When lecturing on Acts, Professor George W. MacRae (1928–85) would emphasize this point by reading the following list. (Whether he composed it himself or got it from someone else, I do not know.)

> Acts includes a wide array of elements, such as a heroic figure taken up in the clouds, followers huddled in a room soon swept through with wind and tongues of flame, the healing of a lame man, people dropping dead for telling lies, prison escapes, an elaborate narration of a lynching, contact with magicians, the story of the conversion of an archrival, plots to kill one of the heroes of the story, raising people from the dead, dreams and visions throughout, the gruesome death of a blasphemous monarch, supernatural guidance and instruction for missionaries, internal intrigues within the movement itself, examples of demon-possessed people who are cured, persons of noble society joining the movement, discussion at a cultural center by one of the

heroes, magical shadows and handkerchiefs, economic turmoil and social unrest caused by the movement, an epic farewell address, frequent ship travel, doom oracles, appeals to the power of Rome, escape from ambush, shipwreck and marvelous escape, and survival after a deadly snakebite. The only element missing is sex!

Who is Jesus according to Acts? Since Acts is Luke's second volume, it is best to follow up on the same three categories that were treated in the section on Luke's Gospel. In Acts, Jesus is the glory of Israel and a light to the Gentiles, a prophet, and a martyr and good example. One of the best proofs for Jesus' resurrection is the success of the movement that he began. Acts provides eloquent testimony to the power of the Holy Spirit that led the apostles to suffer and undertake difficult journeys so that the gospel might reach "the ends of the earth."

Jesus is the glory of Israel and a light to the Gentiles. Just as Luke's Gospel began in Jerusalem with the promise of John the Baptist's birth (Luke 1:5–25), so Acts begins in Jerusalem with the risen Jesus' promise to send the Holy Spirit and then his ascension or return to his heavenly Father (Acts 1:1–11). The apostles' first task is to reconstitute their number to Twelve (because of Judas' defection and death), thus restoring their identification with the twelve tribes of Israel. The gospel goes forth from the Temple city through the agency of the twelve apostles.

The first half of Acts contains several speeches by various apostles (2:14–42; 3:12–26; 4:24–30; 5:30–32; 7:1–53; 10:34–43; 13:16–41). All these speeches refer to Jesus as the fulfillment of Israel's Scriptures. In some cases the reference is brief (see 3:18), whereas in other speeches there is an extensive section of biblical interpretation in which Christ functions as the key to the Scriptures. According to Acts, Jesus' fulfillment of the Scriptures is an essential element in early Christian preaching and so the story of Jesus is never separated from the story of Israel as God's people.

The earliest mission undertaken by the apostles takes place in the shadow of the Jerusalem Temple. In his first summary of the community's life (2:43–47), Luke indicates that "they spent much time together in the temple." Later he notes that "they were all together in Solomon's Portico" (5:12), which was part of the Temple complex. Though persecuted by some Jews, their first missionary successes take place among fellow Jews. The earliest church was a Jewish movement proclaiming Jesus as the glory of Israel.

With the speech of Stephen (one of the Greek-speaking Jews), recorded in Acts 7, the link between Israel's history and the early church is held up to critical examination. After a long rehearsal of Israel's early history, Stephen concludes that "the Most High does not dwell in houses made with human hands" (7:48), that Israel has continually persecuted and killed the prophets sent by God (7:52), and that Israel has not kept God's Law (7:53). The idea is planted that the Jerusalem Temple and a direct connection to historic Israel may not be absolutely necessary to the Christian movement.

Then occur several events that move the gospel beyond Jerusalem. First, Philip in 8:4–40 explains to the Ethiopian eunuch that Isaiah 53:7–8 ("like a sheep he was led to the slaughter") was part of "the good news about Jesus." Then Saul/Paul, once a vigorous persecutor of the Christian movement, receives an experience of the risen Christ and a commission "to bring my name before Gentiles and kings and the people of Israel" (9:15). When the Gentile Cornelius inquires about the gospel, Peter receives a vision from God to the effect that "God shows no partiality, but in every nation anyone who fears him and does what is right is acceptable to him" (10:34–35). And when Greek-speaking Christians arrive from Jerusalem at Antioch in Syria (11:19–26), non-Jews in "a great number became believers and turned to the Lord" (11:21).

When Paul and Barnabas set out on their first missionary journey (13–14), they meet some success (and much opposition) among the local Jewish communities, but much more success among Gentiles—so much so that they discern that God "had opened a door of faith for the Gentiles" (14:27). Finally in the council at Jerusalem (15) all the apostles decide that Gentiles may be accepted as full Christians provided they agree to certain minimal conditions: "to abstain only from things polluted by idols and from fornication and from whatever has been strangled and from blood" (15:20, 29). As Paul continues his missionary journeys, he enjoys his greatest successes among the Gentiles.

In narrating the spread of the gospel in Acts, Luke is careful to root Jesus in the history and life of God's people (the glory of Israel). At the same time, he shows how God led the apostles to see that Jesus is also a light to the Gentiles, thus fulfilling Simeon's prophecy (see Luke 2:32).

Jesus was a prophet. According to Acts, the prophetic character of Jesus' public ministry is continued by the early church. During his public ministry Jesus had been the sole focus of the Holy Spirit's power (see Luke 4:16–30). At Pentecost (Acts 2), however, the Holy Spirit is poured out on all the apostles and disciples gathered in Jerusalem. They become a prophetic community and fulfill the prophecy of Joel: "I will pour out my Spirit upon all flesh, and your sons and daughters shall prophesy" (2:17). In his second speech (3:12–26) Peter stresses that Jesus is the one foretold by the prophets, that he is the prophet like Moses, and that even his suffering was foretold by the prophets. When Peter speaks before the Jewish council, he is "filled with the Holy Spirit" (4:8). Stephen's accusation against his fellow Jews is that they have persecuted and killed the prophets (7:51–52). At several points Luke insists that the gift of the Holy Spirit is an essential element (see 8:14–24; 19:1–6) in baptism, thus making every Christian a prophet to some extent. At the Jerusalem council (15), the momentous decision to accept Gentiles as full Christians and not demand that they become Jews is made first of all by the Holy Spirit: "For it has seemed good to the Holy Spirit and to us to impose on you no further burden than these essentials" (15:28).

Just as one can speak of apostolic succession in Luke–Acts (since the apostles are the principles of continuity between the time of Jesus and the time of the Holy Spirit), so one can speak of a prophetic succession. In Old Testament times God spoke through many prophets including John the Baptist (see Luke 16:16). During Jesus' public ministry he became the sole focus of the Spirit's activities (see Luke 4:18). Now after his ascension and Pentecost, the Holy Spirit is poured out on the community that follows Jesus and spreads the gospel about what God has done in and through Jesus. Because the Holy Spirit empowers and guides it, the church functions as the prophetic community and as the bearer of the Holy Spirit—after the example of Jesus the prophet of God.

The theme of Jesus as an example and faithful witness (martyr) is developed throughout Acts. The Jerusalem apostles do what Jesus did. They preach the gospel, perform miracles, and suffer persecution. In the second half of Acts, Luke seems to be especially conscious of the parallels between Jesus and Paul.

In this way Luke suggests that Jesus' life is a pattern or model not only for Paul but also for all Christians, and that Paul (and every Christian) cannot be understood apart from Christ.

Both Jesus and Paul are prophesied to have special significance for the Gentiles and to be destined to suffer (Luke 2:29–35; Acts 9:15–16). Both Jesus and Paul begin their ministries with a speech in a synagogue that stresses the fulfillment of the Scriptures in Christ and indicates that the mission to the Gentiles is in accord with the Old Testament (Luke 4:16–30; Acts 13:14–52). Both Jesus and Paul are determined to go to Jerusalem where they will be arrested (Luke 9:51; Acts 19:21). Both Jesus and Paul predict their sufferings in some detail (Luke 9:22, 44–45; Acts 20:22–24; 21:10–14). Both Jesus and Paul give a farewell speech that emphasizes the need for humility in Christian service and warns against apostasy (Luke 22:21–38; Acts 20:18–35). Both Jesus and Paul heroically accept their martyrdom as being in accord with God's will (Luke 22:39–46; Acts 20:36–38; 21:5–6, 13–14). And both Jesus and Paul undergo a series of investigations, the effect of which is to establish their innocence with regard to the charge that they are political agitators (Luke 22:47–23:25; Acts 21:27–26:32).

In these many ways, Luke establishes the point that Jesus the faithful witness (martyr) provides the good example and sets the pattern for Christian life not only in Paul's case but also in the case of every Christian.

Questions for Reflection: *How can the church best continue Jesus' dual commitment to Israel and to all the nations? How best can the church fulfill its prophetic mission? Is the Jesus-Paul parallelism a realistic model for Christian life?*

Texts for Special Attention: *Acts 1:6–11; 2:1–13; 2:43–47; 8:26–40; 9:1–22; 17:23–34; 25:6–12; and 28:23–31.*

Chapter 4

The Word of God: John's Gospel and Epistles

On the day before Christmas a few years ago, *The New York Times* ran a front-page story entitled "Pastors Prepare the Hardest Sermon." The point was that most preachers find it hard to say anything new or fresh about the Christmas story. Most people know the Christmas story, and by Christmas eve or morning they may feel they have heard it once too often.

For almost thirty years I have preached every Christmas afternoon. The Gospel text is John 1:1–18: "the Word became flesh and lived among us." That passage does not tell the Christmas story as Matthew and Luke do. Rather, it tells why the Christmas story is important. It tells where Jesus came from

(from God), who Jesus is (the Word of God), and why he came (to reveal God and God's will for us).

John 1:1–18 is the introduction or prologue to John's Gospel. It is like the preface to a book or an overture to a symphony. It introduces the most important themes and ideas, so that we know what to look for in the body of the Gospel. The prologue helps us to make sense of the Gospel as a whole, and the Gospel as a whole helps us to make sense of the prologue.

John's Gospel is different from the Synoptic Gospels. In John there are three Passovers during Jesus' public ministry rather than one. There is a different cast of characters: Nicodemus, the Samaritan woman, the man born blind, Lazarus, the beloved disciple, and so forth. The focus of Jesus' preaching is not the kingdom of God but rather his identity as the revealer of God and the revelation of God. Jesus makes several journeys to Jerusalem, not just one. He gives long speeches, especially at the Last Supper. There are no exorcisms and only a few parables. Though there are links with the other Gospels, the Evangelist for the most part used independent traditions.

The Johannine traditions developed in what is sometimes called the Johannine school, a way of referring to the distinctive early Christian movement in which John's Gospel and Epistles were produced. The Evangelist known as John wrote for a largely Jewish Christian community in the process of being expelled from the synagogue (see 9:22; 12:42; 16:2). In this respect the setting in John's Gospel is similar to that of Matthew's Gospel. The Johannine Jewish Christians regarded themselves as best carrying on the Jewish heritage in the late first century after the destruction of the Jerusalem Temple. Their (fellow) Jewish opponents are called "the Jews."

The Johannine Christians probably lived in the eastern Mediterranean area, though tradition links John to Ephesus in Asia Minor (modern Turkey). The purpose of the Gospel is stated in John 20:30–31: "that you may come to believe (or, continue to believe) that Jesus is the Messiah, the Son of God, and that through believing you may have life in his name." Despite the first translation ("that you may come to believe") it is unlikely that John's Gospel was intended as a missionary tract. Instead, it was probably written to help Jewish Christian believers to adjust to their new context outside the synagogue.

Who is Jesus according to John? He is the Word of God and the Son of God; he is the revealer sent by God and the revelation of God. The proper response to Jesus is to believe (faith) and to love (God and neighbor).

The Word of God (John 1–4)

"In the beginning was the Word, and the Word was with God, and the Word was God." So John's Gospel begins. The prologue identifies Jesus as the Word of God. Just as our words express what we think and want to communicate, so God's Word expresses what God wants to say to us. Jesus is both the revealer of God and the revelation of God. According to John 1:14, God's Word became flesh and dwelt among us as Jesus of Nazareth. The Wisdom of God has become human. That is the basic theological affirmation of John's Gospel.

The entire first chapter of John's Gospel is devoted to identifying Jesus. After the prologue, John the Baptist denies (1:19–28) that he himself is the Christ (Messiah) or Elijah or "the prophet." The reader, of course, knows that Jesus is all of these. Then in 1:29–34 John positively identifies Jesus as "the Lamb of God who takes away the sins of the world," the one in whom the Spirit dwells, and the Son of God. Next in 1:35–42 two prospective disciples address Jesus as "Rabbi" (which means "teacher"), and one of them (Andrew) tells his brother Simon Peter: "We have found the Messiah." Finally, when Nathanael is astounded by Jesus' display of knowledge, he confesses: "Rabbi, you are the Son of God! You are the King of Israel!" Jesus replies that Nathanael will see even greater things, including "the angels of God ascending and descending upon the Son of Man" (1:51). The various sections of John 1 serve to identify Jesus by means of various titles. No one title exhausts the richness of Jesus' person. Each brings out an aspect of the one who is the Word of God.

Chapters 2 through 4 concern the revelation of Jesus and the various responses to him. They begin and end with a "sign" in Cana of Galilee (2:1–12 and 4:46–54). At the wedding feast of Cana (2:1–12) the mother of Jesus shows faith in his power ("Do whatever he tells you"), and as a result of his turning water into wine "his disciples believed in him." There are seven signs in the first half of John's Gospel (2:1–12; 4:46–54; 5:1–9; 6:1–15; 6:16–25; 9:1–12; 11:1–44), which is sometimes called the Book of Signs. These are the equivalents of the miracle stories in the Synoptic Gospels. They are called signs because they point to the deeper reality of Jesus the Word of God.

When Jesus arrives in Jerusalem for the first of the three Passovers in John's Gospel (2:13–25), he makes a prophetic demonstration against the commercialization of the Temple and is perceived as threatening its very existence. John interprets his prophecy ("Destroy this temple, and in three days I will raise it up," 2:19) as referring to Jesus' death and resurrection. Signs are important. But to base one's faith on them alone is not adequate (see 2:23–25); rather, one must believe in the one to whom the signs point.

When Nicodemus (3:1–21), a Pharisee and a leader of

"the Jews," comes to Jesus by night, Jesus tells him that "no one can see the kingdom of God without being born from above" (3:3). Nicodemus misinterprets "from above" to mean "again" (the words are the same in Greek, *anōthen*) and Jesus takes the occasion to instruct him about being born from God and God's Spirit ("from above"). Jesus goes on to summarize the origin and purpose of his own ministry: "For God so loved the world that he gave his only Son, so that everyone who believes in him may not perish but may have eternal life" (3:16).

As in 1:29–36, so in 3:22–36 John the Baptist acknowledges the superiority of Jesus. He first compares himself to the "best man" at a wedding whose main task is to serve the groom. He goes on to describe Jesus as the one who comes from above (3:31) and who is the point of decision (*krisis*) for all human beings: "Whoever believes in the Son has eternal life; whoever disobeys the Son will not see life, but must endure God's wrath" (3:36).

The story of Jesus' encounter with the Samaritan woman (4:1–45) brings Jesus into contact with persons outside Galilee, or Judea, with persons whose Judaism was considered suspect or marginal by "the Jews." When the woman is puzzled that he as a Jew would ask for a drink of water from a Samaritan woman, Jesus promises her "living water...gushing up to eternal life" (4:10, 14). Jesus' knowledge of her past ("you have had five husbands, and the one you have now is not your husband") elicits from her the confession "you are a prophet." The center of the episode is Jesus' declaration that "the hour is coming, and now here, when the true worshipers will worship the Father in spirit and truth" (4:23). This in turn elicits from her the prospect that Jesus might be the Messiah (4:25), a perception that she shares with the other Samaritans whom she brings to Jesus. Meanwhile, when Jesus' disciples return with food, he declares that "my food is to do the will of him who sent me" (4:34). Finally the Samaritans come to believe in Jesus not because of the woman's report but from their own experience: "We know that this is truly the Savior of the world" (4:42).

The final episode (4:46–54) brings Jesus back to Cana. There a "royal official" (most likely a Gentile) asks Jesus to heal his sick son in Capernaum. When Jesus declares that his son will not die, the official sets out for home on the strength of Jesus' word alone and finds that his son has indeed recovered.

The revelation of God in Jesus the Word of God receives both negative and positive responses in Israel: deep trust, hostility, "sign" faith, confusion, and confession. The responses among Samaritans and Gentiles are more positive on the whole.

Questions for Reflection: *What does it mean to call Jesus the Word of God? How do the many titles in John 1 answer the question, Who is Jesus? What is perfect faith in the light of John 2–4?*

Texts for Special Attention: *1:1–18; 2:1–12; 3:31–36; and 4:1–45.*

Jesus and "the Jews" (John 5-12)

John wrote for a largely Jewish Christian community that had experienced the crisis of A.D. 70 and the later expulsion from the synagogue. Before the Jerusalem Temple had been destroyed, it had been the focus of the great Jewish festivals. Without the Temple, how would the traditions embodied in the festivals be carried on? John's answer was that in Jesus the full meaning of the festivals had been revealed. They were signs pointing to Jesus.

The second part of Jesus' public life according to John is structured around the great Jewish festivals: the Sabbath (5:1–47), Passover (6:1–71), Tabernacles or Booths (7:1–10:21), Dedication or Hanukkah (10:22–42), and Passover (11:1–12:50). John uses these festivals as occasions for Jesus to reveal God and his own identity. At almost every point Jesus encounters opposition from "the Jews." Of course, Jesus and all his early disciples were Jews, and so the terms cannot include all Jews. Rather, "the Jews" seems to function as John's way of referring to the opponents of Jesus and (more importantly) to the Jewish rivals of the Johannine Jewish Christian community.

When Jesus heals a paralyzed man on the Sabbath (5:1–47), "the Jews" object to Jesus' command to the man to take up his mat and walk. According to them, that action qualified as work forbidden on the Sabbath. Jesus' response was that God works on the Sabbath: "My Father is still working, and I also am working" (5:17). This answer further outrages the opponents because not only was Jesus breaking the Sabbath but he was also calling God "his own Father, thereby making himself equal to God" (5:18). From the Johannine perspective, "the Jews" are ironically correct in their assessment. As witnesses to his special relationship with God, Jesus calls upon John the Baptist, his own works, his heavenly Father, and the Scriptures (5:31–47).

In John 6, Passover is the occasion for two more signs: the feeding of the five thousand (6:1–15) and the walking on the water (6:16–25). These signs set the stage for the bread of life discourse, which takes as its biblical text Psalm 78:24: "He gave them bread from heaven to eat" (6:31). In his exposition Jesus announces "I am the bread of life" (6:35) and claims that he can satisfy spiritual hunger more effectively than the manna that God provided for Israel in Moses' time or the unleavened bread that Jews eat at Passover in commemoration of the exodus from Egypt. The bread that Jesus gives is himself: "I am the living bread that came down from heaven. Whoever eats of this bread will live forever; and the bread that I will give for the life of the world is my flesh" (6:51).

The Johannine account of Jesus' visit to Jerusalem at Tabernacles or Booths is spread over several chapters

(7:1–10:21). Two of the great motifs of this festival were water and light. And so Jesus proclaims on the last day of the festival: "Let anyone who is thirsty come to me, and let the one who believes in me drink" (7:37–38). And then he says: "I am the light of the world. Whoever follows me will never walk in darkness but will have the light of life" (8:12). The meaning of Tabernacles is fulfilled in Jesus.

The hostility between Jesus and "the Jews" comes to a head over the sixth "sign": the healing of the man born blind (9:1–41). After receiving his physical sight, the man gradually grows in spiritual sight or faith in Jesus. He progresses from regarding Jesus as "the man called Jesus" through recognizing him as "the prophet" and a man "from God" to confessing Jesus as the Son of Man and worshiping him. The "Jews," however, have physical sight but become increasingly blind on the spiritual level and fail to recognize their own blindness. The Tabernacles section ends (10:1–21) with Jesus proclaiming himself as the good shepherd who knows and loves his flock and "lays down his life for his sheep" (10:11).

The background of the feast of Dedication or Hanukkah treated in 10:22–42 is the capture and rededication of the Jerusalem Temple by Judas Maccabeus in 164 B.C. While refusing to answer the question from "the Jews" whether he is the Messiah, Jesus goes further than the title "Messiah" implies and declares: "The Father and I are one" (10:30).

The final sign in the series of seven signs is the restoration of Lazarus to life (11:1–44). Jesus' friend Lazarus had died, but his death was "for God's glory" (11:4). In the course of his conversation with Martha, Jesus proclaims "I am the resurrection and the life" (11:25) and restores the dead man to life. This sign points toward Jesus' own resurrection from the dead. Although many of "the Jews" believed in Jesus because of this sign (11:45; 12:11), the chief priests were planning to kill Jesus out of fear of the Romans. Caiaphas then utters a statement full of irony and truth: "…it is better for you to have one man die for the people than to have the whole nation destroyed" (11:50).

Having been anointed by Mary of Bethany for burial (12:1–8), Jesus enters Jerusalem in a triumphant procession that will issue in his death on the cross. Jesus recognizes what is going to happen and accepts it: "The hour has come for the Son of Man to be glorified" (12:23). The irony is that Jesus' hour of being "lifted up" on the cross (12:34) will be the hour of his return to the Father and his glorification. The cross is a victory and an exaltation, not a defeat.

Questions for Reflection: *What claims does Jesus make about himself in John 5–12? Why do "the Jews" object to Jesus? How does John use irony as a vehicle for truth?*

Texts for Special Attention: *John 5:17–18, 24–25; 6:30–58; 9:1–41; 11:1–44; 11:45–57; and 12:44–50.*

The Son of God (John 13–21)

The passion of Jesus is the hour of glory for the Son of God. That is the basic insight of the second half of John's Gospel, which is often called the Book of Glory as a result.

The Johannine account of Jesus' last meal with his disciples is spread over five chapters (John 13–17). After Jesus washes the feet of his disciples and prophesies his betrayal by Judas (13), he presents several long speeches (14–16) and concludes with a prayer to God as his Father (17).

By washing the feet of his disciples (13:1–20), Jesus not only gives an example of the humble service of others but also interprets his death as his gift to others and asks that his gift of salvation be accepted by Peter and the others. When Judas departs to betray him ("it was night"), Jesus announces the positive significance of his "hour": "Now the Son of Man has been glorified, and God has been glorified in him" (13:31). He also proclaims a new commandment ("love one another") that will mark people as his disciples. This command is based on Jesus' love for the disciples, which is in turn a reflection of the Father's love for him as God's Son.

In his speeches in chapters 14–16, Jesus proclaims that he is "the way, and the truth, and the life" (14:6), the "vine" from whom others receive their life (15:1–6), and the one who has overcome the hostility of the world (16:25–33). The question running through these final discourses is this: How can the movement continue without the presence of the earthly Jesus? There are two basic answers. First, the Father will send the Holy Spirit as the Paraclete (a comforter and defender) to take Jesus' place (14:15–17, 25–26; 15:26–27; 16:7–14). Second, the disciples are to keep "the commandments," which come down to two basic duties: to believe God and his Son and to love God and one another.

The Last Supper ends with the prayer of Jesus as God's Son for himself, for his disciples, and for those who will come to believe through them (17:1–26). In this prayer the Son addresses the Father and provides the correct Johannine interpretation of the passion narrative that follows immediately: "Father, the hour has come; glorify your Son so that the Son may glorify you" (17:1).

John's passion narrative (chaps. 18–19) falls into three main parts: the arrest and hearing before the Jewish high priests (18:1–27), the trial before the Roman governor Pontius Pilate (18:28–19:16), and the crucifixion and death (19:17–42).

At his arrest (18:1–27) Jesus willingly accepts what is going to happen as God's will for his Son: "Am I not to drink the cup that the Father has given me?" (18:11) John also recalls the high priest Caiaphas's plan that "it was better to have one person die for the people" (18:14; see 11:50). These two statements underline the Son's offering of himself and the atoning or expiatory value of his sacrifice.

In the trial before Pilate (18:28–19:16) there is a complex alternation of movements outside and inside, as well as a switching of scenes in which Pilate interacts with either "the Jews" or Jesus. The official charge against Jesus reads "the King of the Jews." For "the Jews" this term evokes the messianic hopes associated with King David, whereas for Pilate it evokes a series of dangerous Jewish political-religious rebels who made trouble for him and his predecessors as prefect of Judea. The central scene (19:1–3) pictures the soldiers' mockery of Jesus as "King of the Jews." The readers of John's Gospel, however, see the irony and the truth in this title being applied to Jesus. They believe that this Jewish teacher from Galilee who has been arrested and mistreated really is the King of the Jews and possesses a kingship superior even to that of the Roman emperor.

The crucifixion narrative (19:17–42) also shows an intricate structure revolving around a central scene: the crucifixion (19:17–18), the request by "the Jews" (19:19–22), the lottery for Jesus' tunic (19:23–24), the central scene at the cross (19:25–27), the death of Jesus (19:28–30), the request by "the Jews" (19:31–37), and the burial (19:38–42). The scene at the cross (19:25–27) features the dying Jesus commending his mother to the care of the beloved disciple: "Woman, here is your son." As God's Son returns to his Father, he takes care that his family on earth (the church) should continue as a community of faith and love. The scene at the cross is both a model for human compassion and a powerful picture of what the church should be. The Son carries on the Father's work right up to the moment of his death.

The death of Jesus is not the end of the story of God's Son. None of the Gospels contains a direct description of Jesus' resurrection. As in the three Synoptic Gospels, John provides narratives about the empty tomb and the appearances of the risen Jesus. The first sequence (20:1–29) takes place in Jerusalem and develops the theme of progress in faith regarding the risen Jesus. The journey moves from Mary Magdalene's confusion to the "doubting" Thomas's recognition of the risen Jesus and his confession "My Lord and my God" along with Jesus' comment "Blessed are those who have not seen and yet have come to believe" (20:28–29). The second sequence (21:1–23) occurs in Galilee and focuses on the church (represented by the disciples) and its mission. Echoing the commission to become "fishers" of human beings, the risen Jesus directs the disciples to make a large catch of fish (153!) and shares a meal with them. Then he elicits from Peter a profession of love and gives him a pastoral charge ("Feed my lambs"). Finally he clarifies the matter of the death of the beloved disciple. Jesus never said that he would not die, only that he might be alive for Jesus' second coming. This disciple may have been the founder of the

Johannine community and the source of its earliest traditions.

Questions for Reflection: *How does Jesus' movement continue according to John? What does it mean to call Jesus the Son of God? In what sense is Jesus' death a glorification?*

Texts for Special Attention: *John 13:1–20; 13:31–35; 16:7–14; 17:1–26; 18:28–19:16; and 20:24–29.*

The Johannine Epistles (1, 2, and 3 John)

In the traditional order of New Testament books, the Johannine epistles appear among the Catholic Epistles. (See chapter 9 for a discussion of the term and a treatment of the other four documents that comprise this group.) The Johannine epistles continue the story of the Johannine community. Whereas John's Gospel was written to help Jewish Christians reorient themselves after the crisis of A.D. 70 and the expulsion from the synagogue, the three Johannine letters deal with problems that arose within the Johannine community in about A.D. 100.

The most substantial and theologically significant of the

Johannine epistles is 1 John. In form it is more a homily or instruction than a letter. Its language and theology are thoroughly Johannine. After a prologue about Jesus as the "word of life" (1:1–4), it deals in turn with God's light (1:5–2:27), righteousness (2:28–4:6), and love (4:7–5:12) among God's children. The epilogue underlines the purpose of the writing: "so that you may know that you have eternal life" (5:13).

First John is a profound treatise on Christian life. It is a reflection on Christian identity in light of the exaltation and glorification of God's Son. It is especially appropriate for the Christmas and Easter seasons because it helps Christians to relate the great mysteries of the incarnation and the resurrection to the practical working out of their faith in everyday life. For Christians, eternal life has already begun ("you have eternal life"), and 1 John is a guide to what that may mean.

First John also helps us to see that there were problems within the Johannine community. The major theological problem involved the humanity of Jesus: "Every spirit that confesses that Jesus Christ has come in the flesh is from God, and every spirit that does not confess Jesus is not from God" (4:2–3). The key expression is "come in the flesh" (see John 1:14: "The Word became flesh"). Some were denying that Jesus really took on human flesh and became one of us. The major practical problem involved sin and its relation to one's status as a child of God: "Those who have been born of God do not sin ... they cannot sin because they have been born of God" (3:9).

These problems were the occasion of division within the Johannine community and of an eventual separation from it: "They went out of us, but they did not belong to us; for if they had belonged to us, they would have remained with us. But by going out they made it plain that none of them belongs to us" (2:19). What precisely lay behind these words we will never know. But at least the verse enables us to recognize that despite all the emphasis on unity there were bitter divisions within the Johannine community.

More light on the life of the Johannine community is shed by 2 and 3 John. They appear to be real letters from "the elder" (the head of the community?) to "the elect lady and her children" in 2 John (to an important woman, or to the church as a whole?) and to someone named Gaius in 3 John. After insisting on the importance of the love command (2 John 5–6), the elder refers to the division and separation mentioned in 1 John: "Many deceivers have gone out into the world, those who do not confess that Jesus Christ has come in the flesh" (2 John 7).

The problem in 3 John concerns a church leader named Diotrephes "who does not acknowledge our authority" (9). The elder is annoyed because Diotrephes has turned away his emissaries. These short letters are reminders that the "golden age" of early Christianity was not free from tensions and divisions within the community.

Questions for Reflection: *What links do you see between John's Gospel and the Johannine epistles? According to 1 John, what does it mean to be a child of God? What was at stake in the dispute whether Christ really "came in the flesh"?*

Texts for Special Attention: *1 John 1:1–4; 2:1–6; 4:7–21; 5:1–5; 2 John 4–6; and 3 John 2–8.*

Chapter 5

Our Lord Jesus Christ: Paul's Letters

About half (thirteen out of twenty-seven) of the books in the New Testament bear the name of Paul as their author. Yet Paul was not a professional writer, still less a professor of theology. Paul was an apostle. He was convinced that God sent him (once a persecutor of churches) to found new churches. The focus of his preaching as an apostle was the gospel from God about Jesus, especially about Jesus' death and resurrection and the benefits for humankind deriving from them.

The six letters treated in this chapter were written by Paul to churches he had founded. These were mainly Gentile churches. After moving on to found other churches, Paul tried to stay in touch with the churches through reports from co-workers and letters. These six letters were substitutes for Paul's personal presence and represent his responses to their questions and problems. In some respects reading Paul's letters is like overhearing one side of a telephone conversation. We do not have access to the reports and letters that had come to Paul from the six churches. And so we are often reduced to trying to figure out what the questions and problems were on the basis of Paul's responses.

Paul writes as a pastoral theologian. He had brought most of his readers to the Christian faith, and the letters were one way of prolonging his pastoral ministry to them. At the same time, Paul treats their problems in light of the gospel, and that makes him a theologian. For the most part the individual community's concerns determine Paul's agenda. And many things that we would like to know about these churches and about early Christian life in general are left untreated.

The six letters are discussed here in their rough chronological order of composition between A.D. 51 or 52 and the late 50s or early 60s of the first century. What is amazing is how quickly Christian faith developed and with what theological sophistication it was expressed.

1 Thessalonians

Paul's first letter to the Thessalonians is the earliest complete document (A.D. 51 or 52) in the New Testament. Paul founded the church at Thessalonica in northern Greece (see Acts 17:1–10) and moved on to Corinth. There he received from Timothy a report about the generally good spiritual condition of the church at Thessalonica as well as some problems that it was experiencing. The letter is Paul's response to the Thessalonians in the light of Timothy's report.

After a greeting (1:1), Paul thanks God for the faith, hope, and love shown by the Thessalonian Christians (1:2–10). Then in 2:1–16 Paul defends his own proclamation of the gospel "not as a human word but as what it really is, God's word, which is also at work in you believers" (2:13). Next in 2:17–3:13 Paul discusses his travel plans and shares news with the Thessalonians. A regular feature of Paul's letters, these reports remind us that Paul wrote as a substitute for his personal presence and as a way of keeping in touch with the communities he had founded.

The Thessalonians also needed advice and encouragement in their efforts at living out their new faith. First Paul in 4:1–12 urges them to pursue genuine holiness and to avoid sexual immorality ("for God did not call us to impurity but in holiness," 4:7) and to show love to one another. The major pastoral-theological problem for the Thessalonian Christians concerned the second coming of Christ and the fate of those who had died before it. The idea of Christ's second coming was part of the gospel Paul had taught them. In 4:13–18 Paul insists that those Christians who have died will share in Christ's second coming by their own resurrection and that they "will be with the Lord forever" (4:17). In the meantime (5:1–11) those who are alive should "keep awake and be sober" (5:6) precisely because the exact time of Christ's second coming is uncertain ("the day of the Lord will come like a thief in the night," 5:2). The letter closes with some rapid advice (5:12–22) along with final prayers and greetings (5:23–28). The entire letter is summarized by Paul's prayer in 5:23: "May the God of peace sanctify you entirely; and may your spirit and soul and body be kept sound and blameless at the coming of the Lord Jesus Christ."

In 1 Thessalonians we see Paul working as a pastoral theologian. He wrote in response to the pastoral problems that his communities faced. He dealt with those problems in light of the gospel—the consequences of Jesus' life, death, and resurrection. The gospel was Paul's supreme authority because it was "God's word...at work in you believers" (2:13).

Belief in Jesus' second coming ("Christ will come again") provides the horizon against which Christian life is lived. The second coming is certain, but its precise time remains uncertain. Therefore Christians are urged by Paul and all the other New Testament writers to be vigilant and on guard as if Christ were to come at any moment. This belief is the context for all the practical advice about Christian life found in this letter as well as the hopeful spirit that should permeate all of Christian life.

Question for Reflection: *In what sense can belief in Christ's second coming be a horizon for Christian life in the present?*

Texts for Special Attention: *1 Thessalonians: 2:1–13 and 4:13–5:11.*

Galatians

Do non-Jews who become Christians have also to become Jews? Do they have to be circumcised as a sign of their incorporation into God's people? Do they have to observe the Jewish festivals and food laws? These were important issues in earliest Christianity. Behind them lay the issue of the nature of the Christian movement: Was it open to all peoples or was it a sect within Judaism? Paul's answers in his letter to the Galatians provided a rationale for the early church to move beyond the confines of Judaism.

Paul had brought the gospel to Galatia, the area in Asia Minor around Ankara in modern Turkey. Those who accepted the gospel were Gentiles, descendants of the Celts who had settled in that area centuries before. After Paul moved on to Ephesus, other Jewish Christian missionaries came to Galatia and insisted that the Gentile Christians had to become Jews by receiving circumcision and observing the Jewish food laws and festivals. Paul objected vigorously and called their teaching a perversion of the gospel of Christ (1:7).

At stake in the letter to the Galatians were Paul's apostleship and gospel, as well as the nature of Christian freedom. And so in 1:1–5 he expands the usual opening formula to insist on the divine origin of his apostleship ("through Jesus Christ and God the Father") and his gospel of freedom ("who gave himself for our sins to set us free from the present evil age"). His usual thanksgiving is replaced in 1:6–9 by a word of astonishment that the Galatians were turning to a "different gospel."

Paul's defense of his gospel in Galatians proceeds on three levels: personal and historical (1:10–2:21), scriptural (3:1–4:31), and practical (5:1–6:10).

Paul had been accused of deriving his gospel from other preachers and of watering down the content. In the personal and historical part of his defense (1:10–2:21) Paul insists that his gospel of justification and salvation for all on the basis of faith came directly from his own encounter with the risen

Christ (1:10–17), that it was approved by the "pillar apostles"—Peter, James, and John—at Jerusalem, and that Peter/Cephas at Antioch had to admit the truth of Paul's gospel that "a person is justified not by the works of the law but through faith in Jesus Christ" (2:16).

The scriptural part (3:1–4:31) of Paul's argument focuses on the figure of Abraham. According to Genesis 15:6, Abraham "believed God, and it was reckoned to him as righteousness" (3:6). Scripture declared Abraham righteous on the basis of his faith or trust in God, before the institution of circumcision (Genesis 17) and before the giving of the Law to Moses on Sinai (Exodus 19–24). Therefore Abraham is the father of all who believe, and faith is the principle of right relationship with God (justification). Since Christ is the fulfillment of God's promise of offspring to Abraham (3:16), those who belong to Christ are Abraham's offspring: "in Christ Jesus you are all children of God through faith" (3:26).

The practical part (5:1–6:10) of Paul's argument develops the conclusion derived from the scriptural part: "For freedom Christ has set us free" (5:1). On the one hand (5:1–12), Paul declares Gentile Christians free from undergoing circumcision and keeping all the provisions of the Mosaic Law. On the other hand (5:13–6:10), Paul encourages them to live in the "spirit/Spirit" rather than in the "flesh," and so to fulfill "the law of Christ" (6:2). Christian freedom means serving Christ and

God as Lord. It does not demand that Gentile Christians become Jews and observe the whole Mosaic Law. By way of conclusion (6:11–18) Paul urges that Christians boast only in the cross of Jesus Christ (6:14).

Paul found in his gospel of justification through Jesus' death and resurrection the rationale for accepting non-Jews into the people of God without demanding that they become Jews. Christ continues the line of Abraham, and faith enables all peoples to become part of Abraham's family. The gospel is the basis for freedom from the whole Mosaic Law and for life in the Holy Spirit (from which good works flow).

Question for Reflection: *What implications does Paul's gospel of freedom have for Christian life today?*

Texts for Special Attention: *Galatians 2:15–21; 3:23–29; and 5:13–26.*

1 Corinthians

Corinth was a seaport in Greece, not far from Athens. Paul had founded a Christian community there (see Acts 18:1–11) and moved on to Ephesus. He had written an earlier letter (see 1 Cor 5:9) and then in about A.D. 55 wrote the long letter known as 1 Corinthians to respond to the problems and questions that had arisen among the (mainly Gentile) Corinthian Christians.

After the address (1:1–3) and thanksgiving (1:4–9), Paul in 1:10–4:21 deals with the problem of divisions within the community. Factions had emerged, with various groups appealing to Paul, Apollos, Cephas (Peter), and even Christ as their "apostle," each claiming a superior wisdom (1:11–12, 17). Rather than asserting his own superiority, Paul appeals to the paradoxical wisdom of the cross and calls on the Corinthian Christians to recall the core of the gospel and to take the cross as the wisdom of God. The various apostles all build on Jesus Christ as their foundation (3:11); in the final analysis the church is God's building and God's temple (3:10, 16).

In chapters 5 and 6, Paul deals with three more problems. He first recommends that a Christian man living with his stepmother be condemned for his immoral behavior (see Lev 18:8; 20:11) and separated from the community, in the hope that he might recognize his error and repent "so that his spirit may be saved in the day of the Lord" (5:5). A second problem concerned lawsuits between Christians (6:1–11). Paul wants them settled within the community rather than in the public judicial system. And finally it appears that some Christians were frequenting prostitutes (6:12–20) on the grounds that "all things are lawful for me" (6:12). Paul rejects this slogan as a misrepresentation of his doctrine of Christian freedom.

Most of the rest of the letter (chaps. 7–16) gives answers to questions asked by the Corinthian Christians. In answer to the assertion that celibacy should be the norm for all Christians ("it is well for man not to touch a woman," 7:1), Paul warns that celibacy is a gift from God (7:7) and urges Christians to remain in their marriages (even with a pagan spouse) if possible. The issue of eating food somehow connected to pagan religious cults (chaps. 8–10) precipitated for some a crisis of conscience but was for others a matter of indifference. Though siding intellectually with the latter, Paul counsels pastoral sensitivity to the former on the grounds that while "all things are lawful," not all things are helpful (10:23).

Questions were also raised about the community's assemblies (chaps. 11–14). Paul directs that women may pray and prophesy in them but must look and dress like women (11:1–16). He insists that the Lord's Supper should be a sign and means of spiritual unity in Christ, not a symptom of social and economic divisions (11:17–34). He contends that the gift of speaking in tongues is the least important of the many charisms manifested in the Spirit-led body of Christ (chaps. 12–14). The highest gift is love, which is described in great detail and beauty in chapter 13.

The last major question concerns the resurrection—Christ's and ours (chap. 15). Some Christians believed they had already experienced the fullness of Christ's resurrection and therefore said that "there is no [further] resurrection of the dead" (15:12). Paul slowed down their enthusiasm by affirming that Jesus' resurrection was "the first fruits of those who have died" (15:20) and that the fullness of resurrection for others remains in the future (15:51–52). He closes in chapter 16 with information about the collection for the Jerusalem Christians, travel plans, messages, and greetings.

For Paul, Jesus is the risen Christ. Nevertheless, the cross of Jesus remains the symbol of Christian faith and the criterion of Christian wisdom. The risen Christ empowers the body of Christ. As part of Christ's body, Christians show forth the gifts of the Holy Spirit and so build up the body of Christ. And the risen Jesus is the pledge of hope in the fullness of resurrected life.

Paul's first letter to the Corinthians shows some of the problems the early Christians faced and some of the questions they had. Paul the pastoral theologian tried to set them straight by appealing to the gospel. He insisted that the cross of Christ is the final authority. He was strict in dealing with some matters (chaps. 5–7) but pastorally sensitive to the consciences of the "weak" in the issue of food sacrificed to idols (chaps. 8–10).

While hardly a systematic treatment of the church, 1 Corinthians supplies important images of the church and teachings about it. The foundation of the church is Christ, and the apostles are God's fellow workers (3:9). The church is God's field, building, and temple. The Eucharist should be a sign and means of unity. The church is the body of Christ and the Spirit-led charismatic community. The collection for the Jerusalem community was a symbol of the unity in Christ that should exist among the Jewish and the Gentile churches.

Question for Reflection: *What theological principles or foundations do you discern at work in Paul's pastoral advice in 1 Corinthians?*

Texts for Special Attention: *1 Corinthians 1:18–25; 3:5–17; 11:17–34; 12:4–11; 13:1–13; and 15:1–11.*

2 Corinthians

Paul's correspondence with the Corinthians was not over. After 1 Corinthians, Paul wrote to them again "out of much distress and anguish of heart and with many tears" (2:4). This "tearful letter" has been lost, unless it now appears as 2 Corinthians 10–13. What happened? Though the details are not clear, it appears that someone or some group at Corinth challenged Paul's gospel and his credentials as an apostle. The question whether Gentile Christians needed to become Jews had surfaced at Corinth (as in Galatia). And there were some criticisms directed to Paul personally that he found particularly painful.

Many biblical scholars regard 2 Corinthians as the most difficult document in the New Testament. Paul is often emotional and elliptical and so the reader needs to supply what Paul left unsaid in his hurry to express himself. The mood or tone changes rapidly from reconciling to confrontational, and back again. And the letter treats many topics. As a result, some scholars consider 2 Corinthians a collection of several short letters written by Paul to the Corinthian Christians, a kind of anthology of Paul's correspondence with them.

An overview of 2 Corinthians indicates that there is some reason to considering it a collection. After an address (1:1–2) and blessing of God because of (and not in spite of) the afflictions that Paul had endured (1:3–11), he defends his integrity ("we behaved ... with frankness and godly sincerity," 1:12), explains the changes in his travel plans, and recalls the pain that someone at Corinth has caused (1:12–2:13).

In 2:14–7:4 Paul defends with great vigor his gospel and apostleship. After affirming his personal sincerity and commission from God, he compares the characteristics of the Old Covenant (letter, death, condemnation, some splendor, veiled and fading revelation) and of the New Covenant (Spirit, life, righteousness, more splendor, unveiled revelation). He concludes that "the Lord is the Spirit, and where the Spirit of the Lord is, there is freedom" (3:17). The implication is that there is no need for Gentile Christians to become Jews.

Rather than focusing on his apostolic successes, Paul points to his sufferings on behalf of the gospel. The extraordinary power of the gospel comes from God, and the gospel is spread by weak instruments ("clay jars") like Paul. What empowers Paul is his participation in Christ's death and resurrection: "always carrying in the body the death of Jesus, so that the life of Jesus may also be made visible in our lives" (4:10). In light of the gospel, life and death become matters of only relative importance. Death means sharing more fully in eternal life, and life on earth means walking by faith and pleasing God (5:1–10).

Paul defines his own ministry as proclaiming the reconciliation made possible through Jesus' death and resurrection:

"In Christ, God was reconciling the world to himself" (5:18). His resumé as an apostle (6:3–10) focuses on the suffering and indignities that he underwent in proclaiming the gospel.

Second Corinthians 8–9 is the first Christian fund-raising letter. The appeal is for the Jerusalem Christian community (8:4). Paul attached great theological and practical significance to this collection. It was an offering from Gentile churches to the mother (Jewish) church in Jerusalem. Paul supplies many reasons why the Corinthian Christians should contribute. The most important reason, however, is the appeal to the generosity of Christ: "...though he was rich, yet for your sakes he became poor, so that by his poverty you might become rich" (8:9).

In the final chapters (10–13) Paul again defends his apostleship. His opponents admit that "his letters are weighty and strong" but contend that "his bodily presence is weak, and his speech contemptible" (10:10). Instead of boasting about his credentials and achievements as an apostle, Paul appeals to his sufferings and personal weakness. While he mentions the former in passing (see 11:21–22; 12:1–4), he puts forward the latter (including his famously mysterious "thorn in the flesh," 12:7) as proof of the paradoxical wisdom of the cross: "power is made perfect in weakness" (12:9).

In defending his gospel and apostleship, Paul's constant reference point is Jesus' death and resurrection. The whole letter is summarized in Paul's affirmation: "I will boast all the more gladly of my weaknesses, so that the power of Christ may dwell in me" (12:9). As a minister of reconciliation between God and humankind (and between Jews and Gentiles), Paul gives voice to what God has done in and through Jesus' death and resurrection: "God, who reconciled us to himself through Christ, has given us the ministry of reconciliation" (5:18). The power of the gospel gives a new perspective on human weakness and suffering, on life and death, and on the old and new covenants. The risen Christ's message to Paul (and to us) is clear but startling: "My grace is sufficient for you, for power is made perfect in weakness" (12:9).

Question for Reflection: *How might reflection on Paul's gospel as presented in 2 Corinthians demand that we adjust our ideas about success and about what is important in life?*

Texts for Special Attention: *2 Corinthians 3:6–18; 5:1–10; 5:14–21; 6:3–10; and 11:23–33.*

Philippians

The first Christian community that Paul founded in Europe was at Philippi in Macedonia (see Acts 16). Paul wrote to the Christians there from prison—at either Ephesus (A.D. 56–57), or Caesarea Maritima (58–60), or Rome (60–62). The mood or tone shifts rapidly, and the subject matter moves around. Like 2 Corinthians, the letter to the Philippians may be a collection of short letters put together in one larger letter.

In the address (1:1–2) to the main letter (1:1–3:1) Paul refers to "bishops and deacons" at Philippi. This is the earliest reference in the New Testament to these offices. In the thanksgiving (1:3–11) Paul introduces the major themes of the letter: joy, sharing and defending the gospel, and overflowing love. Paul shows his great affection for the Philippians; they have been called his favorite community.

Writing from prison (1:12–26), Paul interprets his imprisonment as "for Christ" and for the spread of the gospel. His imprisonment has introduced the imperial guard to the gospel, encouraged his timid allies, and even enlivened his Christian opponents. He faces the prospect of death with perfect faith, confident that Christ will be exalted whether he lives or dies: "living is Christ" (because Paul will continue to preach the gospel) and "dying is gain" (because Paul will be with Christ more fully).

The exhortation to unity (1:27–2:18) is the heart of Paul's letter to the Philippians. He pleads that they "be of the same mind, having the same love, being in full accord and of one mind" (2:2). As a stimulus to unity he urges them to look to the example of Christ the Servant (2:6–11). The description of Christ the Servant is very likely an early Christian hymn that celebrated Christ's self-emptying in becoming human ("taking the form of a slave, being born in human likeness") and in dying on the cross and his subsequent resurrection and exaltation so that "every tongue should confess that Jesus Christ is Lord." This hymn provides a picture of how the earliest Christians regarded Jesus. It also gave Paul the basis for warning the Philippians against "murmuring and arguing" (2:14).

After news about the travels of Paul's co-workers (2:19–3:1a), Paul launches into an attack (3:1b–4:1) against Jewish Christian missionaries who were trying to force Gentile Christians to become Jews. Even though Paul's credentials as a Jew were impeccable, his experience of "knowing Christ Jesus my Lord" made all that seem like "rubbish." The core of Paul's religious experience was being formed with and shaped by Jesus Christ: "I want to know Christ and the power of his resurrection and the sharing of his sufferings by becoming like him in his death if somehow I may attain the resurrection from the dead" (3:10–11). The lordship of the risen Christ and the hope of sharing the glory of his resurrection made it unnecessary for

Gentile Christians to become Jews.

The rest of the letter (4:2–23) urges two women—Euodia and Syntyche—to get along "in the Lord" (4:2–3), counsels joy and peace in the face of the Lord's coming (4:4–7), gives an exhortation to the life of Christian virtue (4:8–9), acknowledges the gift sent to Paul by the Philippian community (4:10–20—perhaps the earliest letter fragment), and sends final greetings (4:21–23).

Paul's letter to the Philippians is an important theological document. The Christ hymn in 2:6–11 is perhaps the oldest source we have for how early Christians understood Jesus. They did so in remarkably "high" terms: preexistence, incarnation, saving death, resurrection, and exaltation. The idea of being "conformed" to Jesus' death and resurrection (3:10–11) points to the core experience that inspired Paul and should inspire all Christians.

What one holds about Christ should in turn shape how one lives the Christian life. Christ the Servant becomes the model and basis for selfless action on behalf of others and for mutual respect within the Christian community. The goal is unity based on the one Christ. And faith in the risen Christ means that death and life can be seen in a new light. Eternal life has already begun. To die means fullness of life with Christ, and to live means the opportunity to share and spread the gospel.

Question for Reflection: *What difference do Jesus' death and resurrection make in the life of the Christian?*

Texts for Special Attention: *Philippians 1:19–25; 2:6–11; and 3:4–11.*

Philemon

Faith in Christ has both theological and social consequences. The shortest letter in the Pauline corpus shows the difference that Christ can make. In the Roman empire slavery was an integral part of the economic and social life. Paul had brought Philemon to Christian faith. One of Philemon's slaves named Onesimus had run away and ended up becoming a Christian under Paul's influence. In his letter to Philemon, Paul writing from prison begs Philemon to take Onesimus back into his household "no longer as a slave but more than a slave, a beloved brother" (16).

After greeting Philemon and his household and "the church in your house" (1–3), Paul thanks God for Philemon's generous and loving spirit (4–7), makes his request that Philemon take Onesimus back (8–20), and closes with travel plans and greetings (21–25).

Paul's letter to Philemon did not end slavery. Indeed, through the centuries it was often used as the biblical warrant for maintaining slavery. And yet an objective reading suggests that in God's eyes all Christians—slave and free—are equal and in the last analysis brothers and sisters in "the Lord Jesus Christ."

Question for Reflection: *In Paul's letter to Philemon, does faith in Christ reinforce or challenge the social institution of slavery?*

Texts for Special Attention: *Philemon 4–7 and 15–18.*

Chapter 6

The Gospel of God: Romans

The word *spirituality* is very popular today. Newspapers and popular magazines regularly report on an upsurge of interest in spirituality. And yet the examples they give generally turn out to be disappointing. What passes for spirituality is often superficial or recreational. There is little substance and almost no carry-over into human activity, beyond feeling relaxed or good about oneself.

The New Testament contains a book—Paul's letter to the Romans—that is the best statement of Christian spirituality I know. Paul tells us how we stand before God in Christ, who we are in Christ, and how we ought to relate to others in light of our relationship to God through Christ. There is nothing superficial about the spirituality that Paul develops in his letter to the Romans.

Paul was the great founder of early Christian communities outside the land of Israel. As he moved on to found other churches, he kept in contact by sending letters to those whom he had brought to Christian faith. Paul, however, did not found the Christian community at Rome. Rather, it arose from within the large Jewish community there.

Paul wrote to the Roman Christians from Corinth in Greece in A.D. 57 or 58. His letter to them is the longest and most systematic presentation of his gospel. Paul wanted to begin a mission in Spain, and so he hoped to pass through Rome on his way. Before that, however, he had to go to Jerusalem to bring the proceeds of the collection for the "poor" Christians there. His letter to the Romans is a request (for lodging and hospitality), pastoral advice (for the Jewish and Gentile Christians at Rome), and an exposition of his gospel (in preparation for Jerusalem and as information for the Roman Christians).

The word *gospel* means "good news." It has a rich biblical background (see Isaiah 40–55) and a place in the Roman imperial vocabulary. In early Christianity it eventually came to refer to the four books about Jesus' life and activity that we call the Gospels. For Paul, however, the word *gospel* referred first of all to the "good news" that is Jesus Christ: "the gospel concerning his Son, who was descended from David according to the flesh, and was declared to be Son of God with power according to the spirit of holiness by resurrection from the dead, Jesus Christ our Lord" (1:3–4). Paul's gospel focused on Jesus' death and resurrection, with little attention to Jesus' teachings and miracles. Paul was mainly concerned with the effects or consequences of the gospel: "it is the power of God for salvation to everyone who has faith . . . in it the righteousness of God is revealed through faith for faith" (1:16–17).

The entire letter to the Romans is an exposition of Jesus as the good news or gospel of God. In chapters 1–4 Paul first explains what the gospel is, why everyone—Jews and Gentiles alike—needed it, and how one becomes part of it (by faith). Next, in chapters 5–8, he reflects on the gospel and freedom—freedom from sin, death, and the Law, and freedom for life in the Spirit. Then, in chapters 9–11, he tries to discern the place of the gospel in God's plan for salvation that involves Jewish Christians, Gentile Christians, and other Jews. Finally, in chapters 12–16, he considers the practical implications of the gospel for Christian life.

Romans is the longest and last of the seven letters recognized by virtually all scholars as having been composed by Paul. Like the other Pauline letters, it is an example of Paul's pastoral theology. It is Paul's most mature, coherent, and systematic exposition of the gospel he preached and called upon to resolve the pastoral problems faced by Roman Christians.

Theologian Karl Barth points us in the right direction in reading Romans as a document of Christian spirituality: "If we rightly understand ourselves, our problems are the problems of Paul; and if we be enlightened by the brightness of his answers, those answers must be ours." Romans offers a grand spiritual vision. It tells us who we are before God through Christ, and how we should relate to others in light of that relationship. Beside it, all other versions of spirituality look small.

The Need for the Gospel (Romans 1–4)

According to Paul, the gospel of God is first of all a person, Jesus Christ (1:3–4). And the gospel has powerful conse-quences—salvation and justification (1:16–17). Paul came to know the gospel and its effects in his experience on the way to Damascus. Through his encounter with the risen Lord, Paul was transformed from a persecutor of the Christian movement to its most zealous proponent.

What changed Paul so dramatically? If we take seriously Paul's own testimony (and we have no other sources), Paul came to see that in Jesus' death and resurrection God made possible right relationship with God (justification). The relationship between God and humankind that had been broken by Adam's sin has been restored even more abundantly through Jesus' death and resurrection. All humans had borne the burden of Adam's sin: "All have sinned and fall short of the glory of God" (3:23).

What broke the dominion of sin and death was Jesus' sacrificial death on the cross: "they are now justified by his grace as a gift, through the redemption that is in Christ Jesus whom God put forward as a sacrifice of atonement by his blood, effective through faith" (3:24–25). Paul came to see Jesus' apparently shameful and cruel death on the cross in a very different light. It was not proof that Jesus was a false Messiah and a troublemaker for the Romans among the people of Israel. Rather, the cross of Christ was a sign of God's love for humankind and the means by which all peoples could know and love God as the Father of Jesus Christ. In short, the death and resurrection of Jesus were and are good news for all humans.

All people needed the gospel. To Jews and Jewish Christians, it was obvious that non-Jews (Gentiles) needed some help from God. And so in 1:18–32 Paul explains why Gentiles needed the gospel. Their fundamental mistake about God led them into ignorance and immorality. Along with other thinkers of his time, Paul assumed that all humans can know God: "For what can be known about God is plain to them, because God has shown it to them" (1:19).

The Gentiles' failure to honor God or give thanks to God led to confusion and idolatry, which in turn issued in immoral sexual conduct ("the lusts of their hearts ... degrading passions ... shameless acts") and in many other evils ("full of envy, murder, strife, deceit, craftiness ..."). The Gentiles' refusal to acknowledge and worship God resulted in their downward spiral of confusion, idolatry, sexual immorality, and all sorts of evil deeds. The Gentiles clearly needed some help from God to get out of their plight. They could not do so on their own. Paul saw Jesus, the gospel of God, as the only solution.

Paul also insisted that Jews needed the gospel. This was less obvious to Jews. After all, Israel was the chosen people of God and had the Law (or Torah) of Moses as their divinely revealed guide. Without denying the privileges of Israel, Paul explains (2:1–3:20) why Jews too needed help from God in the form of the gospel of Jesus Christ. While the Law gave Israel divine guidance and moral superiority, it also imposed on Jews the obligation to live according to the Law: "... all who have sinned under the Law will be judged by the Law" (2:12). While circumcision marks the Jewish male as part of God's people, it is no guarantee of obedience to the Law or of right relationship with God, since "real circumcision is a matter of the heart—it is spiritual and not literal" (2:29).

Both Gentiles and Jews needed help from God in the form of the gospel because "all, both Jews and Greeks, are under the power of sin" (3:9). This claim is backed up by an anthology of Old Testament quotations in 3:10–18 showing that every person and every part of every person needed the gospel. For Paul, sin is not only evil actions. Rather, Sin is a power or force that along with Death exercised dominion over humankind from Adam until the coming of Christ. Through Jesus' death and resurrection, God broke once and for all the dominion of Sin and Death, and made it possible for all humans—Gentiles and Jews—to share in Jesus' right relationship with God.

How do humans become part of this process? Through faith—by imitating the fidelity of Jesus and by acknowledging the saving significance of his death and resurrection: "we hold that a person is justified by faith apart from the works prescribed by the Law" (3:28).

In Romans 4, Paul reflects on Abraham as the model of faith apart from the works of the Law. According to Genesis 15:6, "Abraham believed God, and it was reckoned to him as righteousness." Abraham's faith in God's promise of his son Isaac took place hundreds of years before the gift of the Law to Moses on Sinai and even before his own circumcision (Genesis 17). And so before and apart from the Law and circumcision, Abraham was declared "righteous" on the basis of his faith in God's word. Faith makes Abraham "the ancestor of all who believe" (4:11), Jews and Gentiles alike.

Questions for Reflection: *In what sense is Jesus the gospel of God? Do you find convincing Paul's analysis of why all peoples needed the gospel? Do all people today need the gospel? What is most basic meaning of faith?*

Texts for Special Attention: *Romans 1:16–17; 3:21–26; and 4:16–25.*

The Gospel and Freedom (Romans 5–8)

The gospel of Jesus Christ is the source of genuine freedom. It brings freedom from the dominion of Sin and Death. It gives the possibility to live in the Holy Spirit. Jesus means freedom.

To understand what Paul says about freedom, we need first to recognize some assumptions about God and the world that he shared with other Jews of his time. This worldview is sometimes called modified apocalyptic dualism. It is present in the Dead Sea scrolls and other Jewish writings of the time. According to this perspective, God is the creator and ruler of the universe. The present, however, is a cosmic struggle between good and evil, between light and darkness. The children of light follow the Prince of Light (Michael?) and do the deeds of light. The children of darkness follow the Prince of Darkness (Satan?) and do the deeds of darkness. In God's own time there will be a "visitation" that will mark the vindication of the righteous and the final defeat of the wicked.

Paul and other early Christians (especially John) adapted this schema according to their convictions about Jesus. Paul identified Sin and Death as personified powers with the Prince of Darkness, and Christ and the Holy Spirit with the Prince of Light. Paul viewed Jesus' death and resurrection as the beginning of God's final visitation and as the effective defeat of Sin and Death. Now through Christ it is possible to live in freedom under the Spirit, even though complete freedom will come only with the fullness of God's kingdom.

What are the effects of Jesus' death and resurrection? In 5:1–11, Paul gives a list of some of the effects: justification, peace with God, access to God, the hope of sharing God's glory, the Holy Spirit, salvation from God's wrath, and reconciliation with God. All these are aspects of the relationship with God that Christ makes possible now.

The decisive significance of Jesus in God's plan of salvation is further highlighted by a comparison between Adam and Christ in 5:12–23. Adam's refusal to obey God's command (see Genesis 3) brought about the dominion of Sin and Death: "Just as sin came into the world through one man, and death came through sin, and so death spread to all because all have sinned ..." (5:12). But God's grace manifest in Christ overcame the powers of Sin and Death. Just as Adam's transgression affected all humans, God's grace or favor in Christ affects all even more: "... where sin increased, grace abounded all the more" (5:20). Whereas Adam's sin brought death, condemnation, disobedience, and sin to all humans, Jesus makes possible eternal life, justification, obedience, and righteousness for all who are in Christ.

To be "in Christ" is to share in his saving action through baptism. Paul interpreted baptism as identification with Jesus in his death and resurrection: "Therefore we have been buried with him by baptism into death, so that, just as Christ was raised from the dead by the glory of the Father, so we too might walk in newness of life" (6:4). Jesus' death on the cross broke the dominion of Sin and Death, and made true freedom possible. Jesus' resurrection from the dead made eternal life possible and enables us to live in freedom and walk in "newness of life."

For many people today, freedom means personal autonomy ("no one can tell me what to do"). For Paul, freedom means serving the right Lord, who is God: "But now that you have been freed from sin and enslaved to God, the advantage you get is sanctification. The end is eternal life" (6:22). Only recognition of God (and Jesus his Son) as Lord and the faithful service of God can bring freedom and eternal life.

Romans 7 is a meditation on the lack of freedom that Paul

(and everyone else) experienced apart from Christ. Where Sin and Death functioned as lords, even the Law of Moses, which in itself is "holy and just and good" (7:12), became an instrument for deceiving and enslaving humans. In those circumstances the Law defined sin and stimulated persons to commit sins. To be under the dominion of Sin, Death, and the Law is to live in "the flesh" and to be "a slave to the law of sin" (7:25).

"Who will rescue me?" Paul's plaintive question in 7:24 receives a full answer in Romans 8, Paul's meditation on life in the spirit and the (Holy) Spirit. God's gift of the Holy Spirit enables one to live the life of the spirit/Spirit: "But you are not in the flesh; you are in the spirit, since the Spirit of God dwells in you" (8:9). Being led by the Spirit enables us to live as children of God and to address God as "Abba, Father," just as Jesus did. It gives proper perspective on the sufferings of the present as we look forward in hope for the fullness of redemption. It allows us to pray even when "we do not know how to pray as we ought" (8:26), to trust that God loves us and is for us, and to recognize that we have in the risen Christ a powerful intercessor with God. It emboldens us to confess that nothing can "separate us from the love of God in Christ Jesus our Lord" (8:39).

Questions for Reflection: *What has Jesus done for us? From what and for what did Jesus bring freedom? How does Paul understand freedom?*

Texts for Special Attention: *Romans 5:12–21; 6:1–4; 7:21–25; and 8:1–39.*

The Gospel and God's Plan (Romans 9–11)

Paul was a Jew, just as Jesus was a Jew. And yet Paul believed that just as both Jews and Gentiles needed the gospel, so both could benefit from Jesus' death and resurrection, and share in their positive effects. But not all Jews were accepting the gospel. This fact forced Paul to reflect on the mysterious plan of God in which there are three important entities: Jewish Christians like Paul, Gentile Christians, and Jews who had not accepted the gospel.

Paul could not conceive of a church apart from Israel. Rather, he saw Jewish Christians like himself as forming a remnant within the people of God (see 11:1–6), and as serving as the principle of continuity throughout the history of salvation.

Gentile Christians, according to Paul, became members of God's people through faith in Christ. Their incorporation was the fulfillment of God's promise to Abraham and the proof of God's mercy. What had been "not my people" had become "my people" (9:25). Because of Jesus' death and resurrection God had opened up membership in God's people beyond ethnic Israel: "If you confess with your lips that Jesus is Lord and believe in your heart that God raised him from the dead, you will be saved" (10:9).

The most problematic entity in God's plan was non-Christian Israel; that is, those Jews who had not accepted the gospel. The relative failure of the gospel among his fellow Jews pained Paul greatly: "I have great sorrow and unceasing anguish in my heart" (9:2). Nevertheless, Paul regarded the privileges of Israel within salvation history ("… to them belong the adoption, the glory, the covenants, the giving of the law …, 9:4–5) as still in force. Indeed, at the end of his long and complicated meditation Paul declares that "the gifts and calling of God are irrevocable" (11:29).

How then does Paul explain the Jewish rejection of the gospel? He does so in terms of the biblical images of "stumbling" (11:11–12) and "hardening" (11:25). Israel's temporary failure to accept the gospel was in fact a providential opportunity for the Gentiles to accept the gospel. The Gentile acceptance of the gospel, in turn, Paul believed, would eventually stimulate even more Jews to accept the gospel (see 11:11–16).

The image of the olive tree in 11:17–24 helps Paul to put all the pieces together. The olive tree (a biblical symbol for

Israel) is represented by the Jewish Christians like Paul. The Gentile Christians are the wild olive shoots who have been grafted on to the olive tree. The non-Christian Jews have been broken off the tree. But they can (and will) be grafted back on by God's power.

Paul sums up the entire mystery of salvation in two sentences: "a hardening has come upon part of Israel, until the full number of Gentiles has come in. And so all Israel will be saved" (11:25–26). Without specifying how (through missionary activity, or in God's own way?), Paul affirms confidently that "all Israel" (a collective, or every Jew?) will be saved (when? in history, or at the end-time?).

Questions for Reflection: *Why was Paul so insistent on his identity as a Jew? What implications might Paul's vision of God's plan have for Christian-Jewish relations today?*

Texts for Special Attention: *Romans 9:1–5 and 11:17–26.*

The Gospel and Christian Life (Romans 12–16)

The gospel is not simply an idea. Rather, it is something to be acted upon and put into practice. In the final chapters of Romans, Paul gives general advice for Christian life (12:1–13:14), offers more specific advice for resolving conflicts between Christians (14:1–15:13), and indicates how the gospel was spread (15:14–16:27).

Christian life is an act of worship: "…present your bodies as a living sacrifice, holy and acceptable to God, which is your spiritual worship" (12:1). Because of their relation to Christ, Christians constitute the body of Christ and are empowered by Christ, and so are "members one of another" (12:5). In showing forth the gifts (charisms) of God, they work to build up the body of Christ (12:6–8). Every Christian is gifted by God. These gifts are to be used for the benefit of others, not for self-glorification or personal gain.

In light of the theological foundations outlined in 12:1–8, Paul goes on to give exhortations to love others and to live in harmony with one's enemies (12:9–21; 13:8–10). He urges the Roman Christians to live in harmony also with the officials of the Roman empire by obeying their laws and paying taxes to them (13:1–7). For a very different attitude toward the Roman empire see the book of Revelation. Whether Paul meant exactly what he said or was being ironic, there is no good reason to make Romans 13:1–7 into a timeless and universally valid doctrine of church and state. Rather, it should be regarded as sound practical advice to Roman Christians in the mid-first century A.D.

In 14:1–15:13 Paul addressed a conflict within the Roman Christian community in light of the gospel. The conflict appears to have been between Jewish Christians and Gentile Christians. Christianity began at Rome within the Jewish community. In A.D. 49 the emperor Claudius expelled the Jews (including Jewish Christians) from Rome. In the meantime, Gentile Christians kept alive the Christian movement at Rome. In A.D. 54 the Jews were allowed to return. When they did so, there was an outbreak of hostility between Jewish and Gentile Christians. Who is in charge now?

Paul offered sound pastoral advice to resolve the dispute. He urged the Roman Christians to stop passing judgments on one another (14:1–12), to avoid making others stumble (14:13–23), and to "welcome one another just as Christ has welcomed you" (15:1–13).

The gospel was spread by apostles like Paul (15:14–33) who traveled all over the Mediterranean world to found new communities. The collection that he took up for the church in

Jerusalem was both a sign of and a means to unity among the churches. Moreover, Paul did not work alone. In fact, the gospel was spread by a network of Christians who collaborated with Paul and supported him in various ways. The list of names in Romans 16 is an impressive witness to how the gospel was spread in the early days of Christianity. It included many women (Phoebe, Prisca, Mary, Junia, etc.), Jews and Gentiles, and persons from various social classes (including Erastus, the city treasurer of Corinth).

Questions for Reflection: *What does it mean to be part of the body of Christ? How might Paul's advice in 14:1–15:13 help to resolve conflicts in the church today? How can the gospel best be spread today?*

Texts for Special Attention: *Romans 12:1–8 and 15:14–21.*

Chapter 7

The Head of the Body: Secondary Pauline Letters

Imitation is the sincerest form of flattery. This old saying can help in understanding how most biblical scholars say that six letters attributed to Paul—2 Thessalonians, Colossians, Ephesians, 1 Timothy, 2 Timothy, and Titus—were composed not directly by Paul but by students and admirers after his death. These letters bear Paul's name, since they represent what Paul would have said or should have said in response to later developments in the first century. In that sense they are extensions of the apostle's ministry.

The practice of pseudonymous authorship (that is, writing under someone else's name) was common in New Testament times. Jews attributed books to ancient biblical figures such as Enoch, Moses, and Solomon. Greek and Roman school children learned how to write properly by imitating famous writers of the past. In a culture in which old is good and new is suspect, to adopt the persona of a revered teacher from the past was an honorable literary device.

The six letters written under Paul's name that are treated in this chapter are often referred to as the Deuteropaulines, or secondary Pauline letters. They are judged to be secondary on the grounds of their different vocabulary and style, their different content and theological emphases, and the different historical situations that they presuppose.

Some scholars maintain that one or several or all of the Deuteropaulines were composed by Paul himself. Such judgments merely telescope into the latter years of Paul's ministry what most scholars assign to the entire second half of the first century. There is no question, however, that the Deuteropaulines belong in the canon of Christian Scripture and that they contain important teachings about who Jesus is and why he is important.

The Deuteropaulines focus on the risen Christ (as Paul does), and give particular attention to his relation to and significance for the church. They provide precious witness to how Paul's theology was developed and adapted in the changing circumstances of Christian life.

2 Thessalonians

One of the central topics in 1 Thessalonians was the second coming of Christ. After assuring the Thessalonians that those who had died would not be left out (see 1 Thess 4:13–18), Paul warned that "the day of the Lord will come like a thief in the night" (5:2) and therefore Christians should always be vigilant.

Whether 2 Thessalonians was composed by Paul or a careful imitator, this letter also concerns the second coming of Christ and its implications for Christian life. It contains elements that one would expect in a Pauline letter: an address (1:1–2), two thanksgivings (1:3–4; 2:13–17), a request for prayers (3:1–5), and final greetings (3:16–18). In structure and language 2 Thessalonians closely follows 1 Thessalonians. The author appeals to the apostolic tradition and claims that he (Paul) wrote the letter himself. These features neither prove nor disprove Paul's authorship. It is exactly what a good imitator would do.

The Jesus of 2 Thessalonians will come again to preside at the last judgment (1:5–12). He will come to punish "those who do not obey the gospel of our Lord Jesus" (1:8) and to be glorified by and to glorify those who have believed in him. The last judgment means vindication for believers and punishment for evildoers.

But some were saying that "the day of the Lord is already here" (2:2). The author dismisses such talk as deceptive and describes at some length what must happen first (2:1–12). Another problem was that some other Christians had stopped working in anticipation of the imminent second coming of Christ (3:6–15). The author appeals to the example of Paul who always worked to support himself and advises that "anyone unwilling to work should not eat" (3:10)—a sentence included in the constitution of the former Soviet Union!

The Jesus of 2 Thessalonians is the one who will come again. His coming is certain. When the second coming will be remains uncertain. The author criticizes both those who said that the day of the Lord was already here and those who gave up working in anticipation of its imminent arrival. His message is that Christians should live holy and virtuous lives as they calmly and confidently prepare to welcome the risen Christ as judge and vindicator.

Question for Reflection: *Should Christians fear Christ's second coming?*

Texts for Special Attention: *2 Thessalonians 1:4–12 and 3:6–15.*

Colossians

Colossae was a city in western Asia Minor (present-day Turkey), about a hundred miles east of Ephesus. One can argue that Paul himself wrote the letter to the Colossians on the basis of its language, style, and personal references. If Paul was the author, he wrote from prison (as was the case with Philippians and Philemon), perhaps at Ephesus or Caesarea Maritima or Rome. But there are good arguments that the letter was written about A.D. 80 at Ephesus by an admirer or imitator of Paul: the different uses of certain words or images (especially the body of Christ), the emphasis on the present rather than future dimensions of salvation, and the nature of the crisis addressed (the attractiveness of a mystical or esoteric Judaism). It is better to take the letter as representing what Paul would have said or should have said in response to a situation some twenty years after his death.

After the usual greeting, thanksgiving, and petition (1:1–11), there is a "doctrinal" section (1:12–2:23) that reflects on Christ as the Wisdom of God, Paul as a minister of the gospel, and Christian life as a participation in Christ's death and resurrection. The second part (3:1–4:1) concerns "ethical" matters: a theological foundation, vices to be avoided and virtues to be pursued, and a "household code." The letter ends (4:2–18) with exhortations, travel plans, and various messages.

The key to Colossians is the early Christian hymn about Christ as the Wisdom of God in 1:15–20. The personification of Wisdom was a familiar motif in Judaism (see Proverbs 8, Sirach 24, Wisdom 7). The Christian version of this motif first identifies Jesus as God's Wisdom in the order of creation: "He is the image of the invisible God, the firstborn of all creation" (1:15). Then it describes Jesus as preeminent in the order of redemption: "He is the head of the body, the church; he is the beginning, the firstborn from the dead" (1:18). In him "the fullness of God was pleased to dwell, and through him God was pleased to reconcile to himself all things." Colossians goes beyond Paul's usage, in conceiving of Christ as the "head" of the body and in the emphasis on the cosmic dimension of the reconciliation brought about by Jesus' death and resurrection. Those who recognize Christ as the Wisdom of God and believe in the perfect sufficiency of his reconciling action will not be tempted to seek wisdom elsewhere.

Most of the "doctrinal" section (1:12–2:23) is a commentary on the Christ-as-Wisdom hymn. The basic idea is that since the fullness of God dwells in Christ and since through baptism Christians have entered into Christ's death and resurrection, they have come to fullness in him "who is the head of every ruler and authority" (2:9–15). Christ has made it possible for all to share in the very life of God. No philosophy can do that!

This theological perspective provides the foundation for the "ethical" section (3:1–4:1): "So if you have been raised with Christ, seek the things that are above" (3:1). Participation in Jesus' death and resurrection demands a certain life-style. And so there are vices to be avoided (3:5–11) and virtues to be cultivated (3:12–17)—not so much for self-improvement as for the reason that life in Christ must express itself in appropriate ways. The theme of Colossians is that "Christ is all and in all" (3:11). That theological conviction flows over into Christian behavior, which is always a response to what God has done in and through Christ.

The most controversial part of Colossians today is the "household code" in 3:18–4:1. It takes for granted the social subordination of wives to husbands, children to parents, and slaves to masters. Thus it reflects the social-cultural assumptions of the Greco-Roman world in the first century. And yet even here some fresh ideas are introduced. Each of these relationships is placed in a theological context ("in the Lord"), thus relativizing the authority of the dominant figure (husband, parent, master) and taking the subordinate figures as moral agents in their own right. Moreover, there is an emphasis on responsibilities that the dominant partner has in the relationship: husbands should love their wives; parents should not nag their children; and masters should treat their slaves justly and fairly. Christians today need not embrace the social structures and assumptions of the Roman empire. Nevertheless, the household code's insistences that all social relationships are "in the Lord" and carry mutual responsibilities remain sound corollaries to the affirmation that "Christ is all and in all."

Question for Reflection: *How might the idea of Christ as the Wisdom of God shape Christian life today?*

Texts for Special Attention: *Colossians 1:12–23; 2:6–23; 3:1–4; and 3:18–4:1.*

Ephesians

The letter to the Ephesians seems to have been written not by Paul but by an admirer or student of Paul. The author uses a different language and style, and brings new theological perspectives: the universal church, the apostles as the foundation of the church, and the "mystery of Christ" as the union of Jews and Gentiles in the one body of Christ. The document is more an essay than a letter, and even the address to the church "in Ephesus" is textually doubtful. Nevertheless, its theological outlook is thoroughly Pauline, to the extent that some scholars regard it as a late first-century synthesis of Pauline theology or even as a cover letter or introduction to the corpus of Pauline letters.

After the customary address (1:1–2), there is a long and rich blessing or benediction (1:3–23), a "doctrinal" section about the unity of the church (2:1–3:21), an "ethical" section" about the demands of Christian life (4:1–6:20), and a postscript (6:21–23). The author of Ephesians knew and used the letter to the Colossians, producing a revised and expanded edition of it.

The author of Ephesians was concerned with the church as a whole and as the new humanity in and through which Christ works in the world. The foundation of the church is the apostles and prophets, and stress is placed on the teaching charisms. The unity between Christ and the church is described in and through head/body and husband/wife imagery.

According to 1:20–23 (the end of the long benediction reflecting on what God has done in Christ), the church is the place of Christ's power. The author follows Colossians in insisting on the resurrection, exaltation, and cosmic reign of Christ as the Wisdom of God. Then he connects the lordship of Christ over all creation with the church: "and [God] has made him the head over all things for the church, which is his body, the fullness of him who fills all in all." In the cosmic reign of Christ the church has a central place. It is Christ's power and presence as head of the body that fills the church. The church in turn is the place in which Christ's present reign over all creation is made actual.

Ephesians 2 deals with the reconciliation of sinful people to

God (2:1–10) and with the inclusion of Gentiles in the people of God (2:11–22). Before Christ, Gentiles were not part of God's people and were in a state of alienation from God. But Jesus' death and resurrection made possible a new unity of Gentiles and Jews: "For he is our peace; in his flesh he has made both groups into one and has broken down the dividing wall, that is, the hostility between us" (2:14). Christ has created "one new humanity" and has reconciled both groups to God "in one body through the cross" (2:15–16). Through Christ, both Gentiles and Jews "have access in one Spirit to the Father" (2:18).

The household of God (2:19–22) is built on the foundation of the apostles and prophets, with Christ as the "cornerstone." The image can refer to that stone in the foundation (cornerstone) that defines the shape and structure of a building and gives it sturdiness. Or it can refer to the "capstone" or "keystone"—the topmost stone that completes and crowns a building. Whichever situation we are to imagine, the image emphasizes the pivotal role played by Christ in the church.

The relationship of Christ with the church is developed throughout Ephesians. The writer defines the "mystery of Christ" (3:6) as the inclusion of Gentiles in the body of Christ and the people of God (3:8) and specifies the role of the church as making known the wisdom of God to all creation (3:10). As the head of the body, Christ is the source of all the charisms or gifts of the Holy Spirit that serve to build up the body

(4:15–16). Particular attention is given to the teaching charisms exercised by apostles, prophets, evangelists, pastors, and teachers that insure sound doctrine (4:11).

In perhaps the most famous part of Ephesians (5:21–33), the author develops the husband-wife section of the household code in Col 3:18–19 into a meditation on the relationship between Christ and the church. Starting from the idea of Christ as the head of the body (the church), he portrays the church as the object of Christ's love shown in his self-sacrificing death (5:25), which in turn initiated what transpires in baptism (5:26–27). Marital unity reflects the greater unity that binds Christ and the church.

Question for Reflection: *How does Ephesians contribute to your understanding of the relation between Christ and the church?*

Texts for Special Attention: *Ephesians 1:20–23; 2:11–22; 3:1–13; 4:7–16; and 5:21–33.*

Pastoral Epistles

The three letters addressed to Timothy (1 and 2 Timothy) and Titus are often called the Pastoral Epistles because they address Timothy and Titus as pastors and concern their pastoral duties. Those who defend Paul's authorship emphasize the "personal" details and contend that they were written around A.D. 63–65, during Paul's time of arrest at Rome. Those who deny Paul's authorship point to the non-Pauline vocabulary, the emphasis on different themes, and a historical situation that best fits in the late first century or even early second century. They claim that the Pastorals were composed by a pupil or admirer of Paul, perhaps at Ephesus. The Pastorals are concerned to show how to deal with false teachers causing trouble in Asia Minor, and how Pauline themes and concepts could be applied in the new circumstances.

Following the train of thought in the Pastorals can be difficult. Although some scholars discover intricate structures, most readers get the impression of small units loosely joined together. Some of the small units may go back to Paul himself.

No one can deny that the Pastorals have exercised an enormous influence on the history of the church. They mark a sharp division between orthodoxy and heresy in matters of Christian faith and practice. They provide some of the earliest evidence about church structures and offices. They encourage the fusion of moral virtues and theological virtues and promote the value of good example in drawing people to the Christian movement. They have shaped our ideas about tradition, church authority, and ordination. With their many summaries of Christian faith, they help us to understand how early Christians thought and spoke about Jesus and his significance for us.

1 Timothy

After the address (1:1–2), 1 Timothy consists of a warning against false doctrine (1:3–11), a thanksgiving and a charge to Timothy (1:12–20), instructions about prayer and the community assembly (2:1–15), the qualifications for bishops and deacons (3:1–13), the mystery of Christian faith (3:14–16), predictions of apostasy (4:1–5), the profile of a good minister (4:6–16), the duties of various Christians (5:1–6:2), false doctrine and true riches (6:3–10), and fighting the good fight of faith (6:11–21).

First Timothy (and the other Pastorals) contain several summaries of Christian faith that provide insight into how early Christians regarded Jesus and what they thought to be important about him. According to 1 Tim 1:15, "Christ Jesus came into the world to save sinners." According to 2:5, "there is one

God; there is also one mediator between God and humankind, Christ Jesus, himself human, who gave himself as a ransom for all." According to 3:16, "he [Christ] was revealed in flesh, vindicated in spirit, seen by angels, proclaimed among Gentiles, believed in throughout the world, taken up in glory." These three traditional summaries give eloquent testimony to the focus of early Christian faith in the redemptive power of Jesus' death and resurrection.

Since the content of Christian faith is clear, Timothy the pastor must see that no "different doctrine" is taught (1:3) and that all hold to "sound teaching" (1:10). The mystery of faith is an objective thing to be held onto (3:9), and the church must function as "the pillar and bulwark of the truth" (3:15). It is from the Pastorals that we get the idea of "the deposit of faith" (6:20).

The opposite of sound doctrine is "meaningless talk" (1:6), which proceeds from those who pay attention to "deceitful spirits and teachings of demons" (4:1). The opponents are fascinated by myths and genealogies (1:4) and forbid marriage and demand abstinence from certain foods (4:3). In the Pastorals there is a clear line between the sound doctrines of the Pauline tradition and the false doctrines of the false teachers.

As part of the response to the false teachers, 1 Timothy places strong emphasis on local church officers. Whereas in Paul's day the apostle who went from place to place was the key figure, by the time of the Pastorals there was a need to promote and encourage local leadership, in order to provide greater stability and direction for the churches. The list of qualifications for bishops and deacons (3:1–13) emphasizes good natural qualities and external respectability. Timothy is said to have received his gift (charism) as pastor "through prophecy with the laying on of hands by the council of elders" (4:14). There is also an officially recognized order of widows with carefully prescribed entrance requirements (5:3–16). Finally, 5:17–22 lists rules for elders or presbyters concerning their salary, procedures to be followed when they are accused of sin, and their evaluation before ordination.

The ideal of Christian life is "a pure heart, a good conscience, and sincere faith" (1:5) and "a quiet and peaceable life in all goodness and dignity" (2:2). There is much emphasis on external respectability for all Christians, who are assumed to be an integral part of Greco-Roman society. Women are to perform good deeds (2:10), be silent in the assembly (2:11), and bear children (2:15). That Christians might own slaves (6:1–2) and amass great wealth are taken for granted.

Question for Reflection: *In what ways has the pastoral advice in 1 Timothy influenced church history and Christian life?*

Texts for Special Attention: *1 Timothy 2:5–6; 3:1–7; 3:14–16; and 6:11–16.*

2 Timothy

Following the address (1:1–2), 2 Timothy presents a thanksgiving and charge to Timothy (1:3–18), the profile of the good minister (2:1–26), the picture of the evildoers in the last days (3:1–9), a final charge to Timothy (3:10–4:8), and personal instructions and greetings (4:9–22). The same emphasis on the content of Christian faith, local ministers, and external respectability based on the practice of virtue appears in 2 Timothy.

There is a summary of the gospel: "Remember Jesus Christ, raised from the dead, a descendant of David" (2:8). And there is what was probably part of a baptismal formula: "If we have died with him, we will also live with him; if we endure, we will also reign with him; if we deny him, he will also deny us; if we are faithless, he remains faithful—for he cannot deny himself" (2:11–13). These formulas echo Paul's summary of the gospel in Romans 1:3–4 and Paul's teaching on baptism in Romans 6:1–4.

Again there is a sharp difference between "the standard of sound teaching" (1:13) and the "profane chatter" of the opponents (2:15). These opponents claim that "the resurrection has already taken place" (2:18; see 1 Cor 15:12). The comparison of them to Jannes and Jambres (3:8; see Exod 7:11) suggests an interest in magic. Timothy, however, is instructed to guard the deposit of faith ("the good treasure entrusted to you," 1:14) and to hand on what he heard from Paul "to faithful people who will be able to teach others as well" (2:2). Implied here is the idea of the transmission of an original revelation by authorized persons who are charged with keeping it intact.

Timothy the pastor received his ministry (which is also his charism) "through the laying on of my [Paul's] hands" (1:6). Here charism and ministry are joined, and the imposition of hands (as a rite of ordination) becomes part of the public ratification of Timothy's charism.

It is understood that God will provide Timothy with whatever is necessary for carrying out his ministry ("a spirit of power and of love and of self-discipline," 1:7). Whereas the opponents hold to only "the outward form of godliness" (3:5), Timothy is urged to pursue righteousness, faith, and peace (2:22). His external respectability is solidly based on the practice of the Christian virtues.

Question for Reflection: *How would the emphases in 2 Timothy (and the other Pastorals) have combated the opponents? Are these emphases helpful for the church today?*

Texts for Special Attention: *2 Timothy 2:1–7; 3:10–17; and 4:1–8.*

Titus

After the salutation (1:1–4), the letter to Titus deals with Titus's work on Crete (1:5–16), teaching sound doctrine (2:1–15), good deeds (3:1–11), and personal instructions and final greetings (3:12–15). That an early Christian summary of faith has been integrated into 3:4–7 is suggested by what follows: "The saying is sure" (3:8). The summary must have been associated with baptism: "through the water of rebirth and renewal by the Holy Spirit." The theology is thoroughly Pauline: "he saved us, not because of any work of righteousness we had done … so that having been justified by his grace, we might become heirs according to the hope of eternal life."

In 1:5–9, Titus is charged with setting up church structures on the island of Crete. He is to appoint elders, and (from the board of elders?) he is to choose a bishop who is respected not only for his natural virtues but also for his firm grasp on the gospel and ability "to preach with sound doctrine and to refute those who contradict it" (1:9). Titus himself is to teach "what is consistent with sound doctrine" (2:1).

The opponents on Crete seem to have been much like those encountered by Timothy in Ephesus. They propagate Jewish myths and food laws (1:14–15), and are said to be interested in speculations, genealogies, and disputes about the Law

(3:9). They are accused of being idle talkers and deceivers and seeking their own "sordid gain" (1:10–11). Good Christians should avoid such persons.

The moral teaching of the letter to Titus blends the moral virtues of Greek philosophy and the distinctively Christian virtues. In the household code (2:1–15) there are instructions for older men and women and for younger men and women, as well as for slaves. There are calls to pursue temperance, prudence, and justice and also to work at faith, love, and hope. One important motive for cultivating the life of virtue is that "the word of God may not be discredited" (2:5) and that opponents may have "nothing evil to say of us" (2:8). This is the missionary strategy of good example that was (and is) so effective in drawing people to the church.

Question for Reflection: *How do you understand the relation between Christian faith and morality?*

Texts for Special Attention: *Titus 1:5–9; 2:11–14; and 3:4–7.*

Chapter 8

The High Priest: Hebrews

"A reading from Paul's Letter to the Hebrews." You may have heard that statement more than once in church. In fact, every part of it is wrong. Hebrews was not written by Paul. It is not a letter. And it is not to the Hebrews.

It does not require much familiarity with Paul's letters and the secondary Pauline letters to recognize that Paul did not write Hebrews. The language and style, the modes of argument, and the theological concerns are very different.

Only the last few verses (13:22–25) might lead one to identify Hebrews as a letter. In fact, they probably represent a note attached by the author as he sent off his work. The body of Hebrews is a sermon or homily on Christ the high priest. As a good sermon, it combines scriptural exposition and moral exhortation.

Those addressed by this sermon are Christians. They may well have been Jews who had become Christians and were in danger of falling away. Since so much attention is given to the Old Testament and its interpretation, it seems natural that Jewish Christians would have been most interested and impressed by biblical arguments. And the exhortations are especially concerned with the theme of holding firm to Christian faith.

The primary concern of Hebrews is the absolute superiority of Christ the high priest. He is the new word of God (chaps. 1–4), the great high priest (chaps. 5–10), and the model of faith (chaps. 11–13). The most distinctive theological concept in Hebrews is the high priesthood of Christ. This idea takes its starting point from two concepts that were commonly accepted in early Christianity: Jesus' death was a sacrifice "for us" and "for our sins," and Jesus willingly went to his death on the cross in accord with God's will. A priest offers sacrifices. In this interpretation of Jesus' death, Jesus the high priest willingly offered his life as a sacrifice for sins. And so he is both the sacrifice and the one who made the sacrifice. Hebrews then is a long sermon about the nature of Jesus' death and its implications for Christian life.

It is important to recognize at the start that the author of

Hebrews is talking about the priesthood of Christ and not directly about the Christian ministerial priesthood (as a church office) or about the priesthood of God's people. It is possible to read Hebrews either as rendering all other priesthoods obsolete or as providing the shape of the Christian priesthood. The author's real concern, however, was the priesthood of Christ as a way of understanding Jesus' death on the cross.

By whom, when, and where Hebrews was written remain mysteries. The Church Father Origen said that only God knows who wrote Hebrews. The author's treatment of Scripture and occasional use of philosophical terminology suggest Alexandria in Egypt as the place of composition, though the postscript (13:22–25) indicates some connection with Italy. The absence of any reference to the destruction of the Jerusalem Temple in A.D. 70 may be significant, since the historical end of the Temple sacrifices would have added to the argument. But a date anywhere between A.D. 60 and 95 (when it was cited in *1 Clement* 36) is possible.

The New Word of God (Hebrews 1–4)

The first four verses (1:1–4) serve as a prologue or introduction to the sermon's major themes: the incompleteness of the Old Testament's revelation and the superiority of God's revelation in Christ, Jesus as the Wisdom and Word of God ("the reflection of God's glory and the exact imprint of God's very being"), the salvific effect of Jesus' death ("purification for sins") and his subsequent exaltation ("he sat down as the right hand of the Majesty on high"), and the absolute superiority of God's Son even to the angels ("the name he has inherited is more excellent than theirs").

The first item on the author's agenda is the last item mentioned in the prologue: the superiority of God's Son to the angels (1:5–14). There is some evidence in contemporary Judaism for the idea of salvation as sharing the life of the angels and in early Christianity for an angel Christology. But whether the author was combating a specific belief or group is not clear. What is clear is the mode of his argument. A chain or catena of biblical quotations (taken out of context) are understood as addressed by God to Christ as God's Son. The most famous texts are Psalm 2:7 ("You are my Son; today I have begotten you," Heb 1:5), and Psalm 110:1 ("Sit at my right hand," Heb 1:13). The point is that angels are servants of God (1:14), whereas Jesus Christ is the Son of God.

Good sermons blend biblical interpretation and exhortation. And so in 2:1–4 the author warns his audience against drifting away and neglecting "so great a salvation."

The second biblical section (2:5–9) takes Psalm 8:4–6 as its text. The biblical psalm was a meditation on the great dignity of humankind ("the son of man"). The author of Hebrews, however, identifies the "son of man" with Jesus and assumes that Psalm 8 was really talking about Jesus. For him, Jesus Christ is the key to the Scriptures. Therefore, when the psalm spoke about being "for a little while lower than the angels," it was describing Christ's incarnation and especially his passion and death. And when the psalm spoke of his being crowned "with glory and honor" and having everything subjected to him, it was really describing the resurrection and exaltation of Christ.

The theological reflection in 2:10–18 introduces some of the most important themes of the sermon. Christ is the "pioneer" of salvation, the one who takes the lead and goes before us (2:10). Christ is the "merciful and faithful high priest" who makes "a sacrifice of atonement for the sins of the people" (2:17). This is the fundamental insight of Hebrews: Christ is both the priest and the sacrifice. And by his suffering, Christ shows his kinship with humankind and so is able to help "those who are being tested." The humanity of Christ is made manifest in his suffering, and because he suffered he can show compassion to other humans.

If Christ is superior to the angels, he is also superior to Moses (3:1–6). The author takes Numbers 12:7 as his biblical text: Moses "was faithful in all God's house." The implication is that Moses was a servant in God's house. The house belongs to God as its builder and to the builder's son (Christ). Just as in a human household a son is superior to a servant, so in God's household (all creation) Christ the Son is superior to Moses the servant.

One of the most sustained examples of biblical interpretation in Hebrews concerns the wandering people of God (3:7–4:11). The biblical text is Psalm 95:7–11: "Today, if you hear his voice … " The passage describes ancient Israel's wandering in the wilderness after the exodus and before its entry in the land of Canaan. In its wanderings in the wilderness Israel rebelled against God and tested God's patience. God grew angry at the people and swore that they would never find rest in the land of Canaan.

In his exposition the author first reflects on the unfaithfulness of the exodus generation (3:12–19). Because of their disobedience and unbelief the exodus generation (apart from Joshua and Caleb) was not allowed to enter the promised land.

But Psalm 95 also speaks a warning to Christians, lest they "turn away from the living God" (3:12) and fail to enter God's rest. Then in 4:1–5 the author considers the faithfulness required of Christians. In contrast with the "unbelief" shown by the exodus generation, those who do believe God's word may enter into "rest." The true rest, however, is not the land of Canaan. Rather, it is a share in God's own life in heaven—God's Sabbath rest. The exposition ends in 4:6–11 with an exhortation to recognize "today" that "a Sabbath rest still remains for the people of God" (4:9). Whereas the exodus generation provided a negative example of disobedience and unbelief, it is still possible for the Christian community as God's pilgrim people to find perfect rest with God.

The first part of Hebrews ends with a reflection on God's word (4:12–13) and a transitional exhortation about Jesus as the Son of God and high priest (4:14–16). The "word of God" in 4:12–13 is first of all the Scriptures—what we call the Old Testament. When properly interpreted with Christ as their key, the Scriptures (as in the case of Psalm 95) speak to us "today" and truly are "living and active, sharper than any two-edged sword." Before God "all are naked and laid bare"—note the transition from God's word to God, and recall that the whole section began by identifying Jesus as God's Word (1:1–4; see John 1:1–18; Col 1:15–20).

The transitional exhortation (4:14–16) introduces the

main theme of chapters 5–10: the priesthood of Christ ("we have a great high priest"). Through his resurrection and exaltation, Christ now resides with God in heaven and serves as a mediator with God for us. Therefore Christians on earth should hold fast to their confession of faith and approach God ("the throne of grace") with confidence and boldness.

Questions for Reflection: *In what sense is Christ superior to the angels and to Moses? How can Jesus be called a priest? What significance might the exposition of Psalm 95 (Heb 3:7–4:11) have for the church today?*

Texts for Special Attention: *Hebrews 1:1–4; 3:7–4:11; and 4:14–16.*

The Great High Priest (Hebrews 5–10)

What makes Jesus a priest? Surely not his human lineage. He was from the tribe of Judah through David, not from the descendants of Aaron and Levi. Priesthood in ancient Israel was based first of all on one's lineage (through tribe, clan, and family) rather than on the response to a special calling from God. According to that criterion, Jesus did not qualify as a priest and still less as the high priest.

In 5:1–10 the author first reflects on the qualifications of priests (not only Jewish priests but also pagan priests) and then shows how Jesus met those qualifications. A priest is chosen from among humans, offers sacrifices for their sins and for his own sins, and is ultimately called by God (5:1–4). Then the author shows how Jesus fulfilled this definition of priesthood. Moving in reverse order in 5:6–10, he establishes that Jesus was called by God on the basis of Psalm 2:7 and 110:4, that through his suffering he was able to sympathize with sinners, and that he became for God's people "the source of eternal salvation for all who obey him." The priesthood of Jesus is not that of Aaron and Levi. Rather, it is the priesthood of Melchizedek, an idea to be developed at length in Hebrews 7.

Before turning to biblical interpretation to ground the priesthood of Jesus, the author offers an exhortation in 5:11–6:20. He first (5:11–6:3) challenges his audience to move beyond the basics of Christian doctrine and go forward toward perfection. Then in 6:4–8 he warns them that "it is impossible to restore again to repentance those who have once been enlightened . . . and then have fallen away." If his original audience was indeed made up of Jewish Christians who were tempted to give up Christianity and return to Judaism, this was a very serious threat.

In 6:9–20, however, he seems confident "of better things in your case." The ground of his hope and of their hope is Jesus who has already entered into the fullness of life with God as a "forerunner on our behalf" (6:20). The pilgrim people of God has a leader, a pioneer, "one who has gone before us and now intercedes with God on our behalf and shows the way in the present time of testing." Here as elsewhere, the exhortation has its theological foundation in Christ's death and resurrection.

The meditation on the priesthood of Christ after the pattern of Melchizedek (7:1–28) takes as its starting point the only two references to Melchizedek in the Old Testament. We have already seen Psalm 110:4 in Heb 5:6: "You are a priest forever, according to the order of Melchizedek." The other passage is Genesis 14:17–20, which describes the encounter between Melchizedek and Abraham. In the introduction to the meditation (7:1–3) the author uses the silence of the latter text about Melchizedek's origin and death ("without father, without mother, without genealogy, having neither beginning of days nor end of life") to establish the eternal character of Christ's priesthood on the basis of the former text ("a priest forever").

Then in 7:4–10 the author establishes the superiority of the priesthood of Melchizedek (and so of Christ) over the Levitical priesthood. According to Genesis 14:17–20, Abraham gave a tithe to Melchizedek, the priest-king of Salem (Jerusalem), who in turn blessed Abraham. Now it is usual that the inferior figure pays the tithe and receives a blessing. Therefore in this case Melchizedek is the superior and Abraham is the inferior. Levi was a descendant of Abraham. And so according to the author's logic the priesthood of Melchizedek (and of Christ) is superior to that of Levi (the Jewish priesthood).

According to 7:11–19, a new priesthood demands a new law. The author admits that Jesus from the tribe of Judah had no claim to the Jewish priesthood of Aaron and Levi. But God has made Jesus a priest, since he is both the perfect sacrifice and the priest who offered the sacrifice (his atoning death). The confirmation and ground of Jesus' priesthood is his resurrection ("through the power of an indestructible life"). Jesus' priesthood is eternal (7:20–25) because God has sworn: "You are a priest forever" (Ps 110:4). Because of Jesus' resurrection, his priesthood continues forever and remains the same, whereas other priests live and die.

The essence of Christ's priesthood is expressed in 7:27: "Unlike the other high priests, he has no need to offer sacrifices day after day, first for his own sins, and then for those of the people; this he did once for all when he offered himself." His sacrifice—his death on the cross—was the one perfect sacrifice for sins. Therefore there is no further need for other atoning sacrifices. Moreover, his resurrection and exaltation made Jesus who willingly gave his life the eternal high priest with God in heaven. Therefore there is no further need for the Levitical priesthood on earth. The priesthood of Christ is a function of his atoning death and resurrection.

From this description of the priesthood of Christ there flows a lengthy treatment of worship and covenant in Hebrews 8–10. The oppositions between heaven and earth, new and old, and spiritual and material serve to contrast the new spiritual lordship and covenant of Christ and the old material worship of the Levitical priests carried out under the old covenant.

Jesus now functions as high priest in the heavenly sanctuary ("the true tent"), of which the earthly sanctuary was only "a sketch and shadow" (8:1–5). He is the mediator of a "better covenant" based on better promises. This is in fact the new covenant promised by the prophet Jeremiah (31:31–34), which has rendered obsolete the old covenant. Whereas worship at the earthly sanctuary in Israel was material, the worship now offered by Christ in "the Holy Place" (heaven) has no need of furniture and animals. The one perfect sacrifice ("the blood of Christ") has been offered by Christ himself to God (9:1–14).

The basis of the new covenant is the death of Jesus (9:15–22). Just as a will (or testament) takes effect only at death, so the new covenant (testament) has been inaugurated by Jesus' death. Likewise, his perfect sacrifice means the end of the old order of sacrifices in the earthly sanctuary (9:23–28): "… he has appeared once for all at the end of the age to remove sin by the sacrifice of himself."

That the Old Testament Law was "only a shadow of the good things to come" is indicated by its rules that material sacrifices (animals, cereals, etc.) should be offered in the earthly sanctuary "year after year" (10:1–18). By contrast, "we have been sanctified through the offering of the body of Jesus Christ once for all" (10:10). The same point is made later by the statement "when Christ had offered for all time a single sacrifice for sins" (10:12). Both statements summarize the theology of Hebrews.

As in 5:11–6:20, the concluding exhortation (10:19–39) combines encouragement and warning. The warning (10:26–31) is not to persist in sin after having received knowledge of the truth. The encouragement is again based on faith in the atoning power of Jesus' death, which allows Christians to approach God "with a true heart in full assurance of faith."

Questions for Reflection: *Why can Jesus be a priest? What does Jesus' priesthood have to do with his resurrection? Why should Christians take encouragement from his death and resurrection?*

Texts for Special Attention: *Hebrews 5:1–10; 7:1–28; and 9:23–28.*

Model of Faith (Hebrews 11–13)

Those Christians who were originally addressed in Hebrews were apparently wavering in their commitment to Christ and contemplating a return to Judaism. They seem also to have endured suffering: "You endured a hard struggle with sufferings" (10:32). In the last part of his sermon, the author directly confronts the themes of faith and suffering.

The encomium on faith in Hebrews 11 is one of the book's most famous parts. It first defines faith as "the assurance of things hoped for, the conviction of things not seen" (11:1). Then it reflects on how great figures of the Old Testament—Abel, Enoch, Noah, Abraham, Isaac, Jacob, Joseph, Moses, and so forth—displayed this kind of faith to put up with suffering in their search for perfection. And yet those models of faith remained "strangers and foreigners on the earth " (11:13) and continued "seeking a homeland…a better country, that is, a heavenly one" (11:14, 16). They still "did not receive what was promised" (11:32).

The great biblical models of faith pointed toward the one great model of faith, Jesus Christ. He is aptly called "the pioneer and perfecter of our faith" (12:2). Like them, he endured suffering for his faith (the cross) and was rewarded with the perfect rest of eternal life with God (resurrection and exaltation). The example of Jesus in turn should encourage those who are growing weary or losing heart, as was the audience first addressed in Hebrews: "In your struggle against sin you have not yet resisted to the point of shedding blood" (12:4).

The appeal to follow the example of Jesus is followed in 12:5–13 by a reflection on the educative value of suffering (suffering as a discipline). Taking his text from Proverbs 3:11–12 ("the Lord disciplines those whom he loves"), the author urges his audience to accept their present suffering as a child accepts discipline from a loving parent. Such suffering is only temporary, and its results are in the end positive ("it yields the peaceful fruit of righteousness"). Having put their sufferings in proper perspective, the author can encourage his wavering and suffering audience to "lift up your drooping hands and strengthen your weak knees, and make straight paths for your feet" (12:12–13). In other words, they are urged to take their place again among the pilgrim people of God and move forward with renewed confidence on their way to perfect rest.

The sermon (or letter) ends with pastoral exhortations (12:14–13:25). The author reminds his audience with what great mysteries they have come into contact by becoming Christians: the heavenly Jerusalem, the court composed of angels and saints, God the judge of all, and Jesus "the mediator of a new covenant" (12:24). He warns them once more against backsliding, using the example of Esau who "found no chance to repent" (12:17). And he points forward to the great end-time event: "Yet once more I will shake not only the earth but also the heaven" (12:26). He has already established on the basis of the priesthood of Christ that for the faithful the last judgment will be a vindication rather than a cause for fear: "so Christ, having been offered once to bear the sins of many, will appear a second time, not to deal with sin, but to save those who are eagerly waiting" (9:28).

In the meantime, Christian life on earth should be characterized by hospitality to strangers, visiting those in prison, chaste marriages, and contentment with modest material wealth (13:1–6). Two calls to respect and obey church leaders (13:7 and 13:17–19) are interrupted by a new interpretation of the Old Testament's sacrificial system. With the one perfect sacrifice of Christ ("to sanctify the people by his own blood," 13:12), there is no longer need for food laws or animal sacrifices. Now the acceptable sacrifice offered by God's people (13:15–16) consists in confessing God's name ("a sacrifice of praise to God") and doing good deeds ("such sacrifices are pleasing to God"). The sermon ends with a benediction (13:20–21) and greeting appropriate to a letter (13:22–25).

Questions for Reflection: *In what sense is Christ the perfect model of faith? How do you react to the idea of suffering as a divine discipline? How can the biblical idea of sacrifice inform Christian life today?*

Texts for Special Attention: *Hebrews 11:8–19; 12:1–13; and 13:8–16.*

The Chief Shepherd: Catholic Epistles

The Catholic Epistles—James; 1 and 2 Peter; 1, 2, and 3 John; and Jude—are the most neglected documents in the New Testament. They are short and do not compare in theological richness (except perhaps 1 Peter) with John's Gospel or Paul's letter to the Romans. In the development of the canon of Christian Scriptures, these seven letters were often on the margin and accepted only gradually and not without debate regarding their apostolic origin and content.

The term *catholic* (which means "universal, general") refers to the eventual acceptance of these seven letters by all the churches of the East and West. It also testifies to the conviction that they contain general advice that is useful for all the churches. Finally it suggests that they can contribute to our understanding of some important features in the development of a *catholic* (in the sense of universal or worldwide) church.

The Johannine letters (1, 2, and 3 John) have already been treated with John's Gospel, since they continue the history of the Johannine community. Here we treat James, 1 Peter, Jude, and 2 Peter. Most scholars regard these letters as pseudonymous; that is, written under the name of a famous figure of the apostolic generation. As in the case of the secondary Pauline letters, these documents present what the apostle would have said or should have said in the new situation of the late first century.

Short, marginal, and of dubious origin—these characteristics explain why the Catholic Epistles get little attention. Yet they can still make important contributions to our understanding of Jesus and his significance for Christian life. James is the best New Testament resource for teachings on social justice. First Peter takes up the issue of innocent suffering. And Jude and 2 Peter (a second edition of Jude) bear witness to the growing significance of the "apostolic faith." As in the Pauline epistles, we hear only one side of a conversation, and so it is hard to know what the "Pauline" opponents in James or the "heretics" in Jude and 2 Peter were really saying or what the precise nature of the persecution in 1 Peter was. The expression "Chief Shepherd" as a title for Christ appears in 1 Peter 5:4. Here it refers to the pastoral advice that the Catholic Epistles provide, each in its own distinctive way.

James

The only feature to suggest that James is a letter is in the opening verse: "James...to the twelve tribes...Greetings." There is no evidence in the rest of the book for a specific situation that may be addressed by a letter. And there are no further greetings, messages, or travel news. James is better understood as a wisdom instruction than as a letter.

The wisdom instructions in the Old Testament—Proverbs, Sirach, and Ecclesiastes—join together general ethical comments on various topics. It is usually difficult to discern in them a clear outline or progress of thought. They are more like anthologies than linear arguments. James fits into this category. After the "letter" address (1:1), it deals with various themes (1:2–18), hearing and doing (1:19–27), partiality (2:1–13), faith and works (2:14–26), the tongue (3:1–12), contentiousness (3:13–4:12), rich and poor (4:13–5:6), and various themes (5:7–20). Even this outline suggests more logical coherence than is to be found on reading the book straight through.

Who is James? In 1:1 the author describes himself as "a

servant of God and of the Lord Jesus Christ." He is usually taken to be James "the brother of the Lord" (see Mark 6:3; Matt 13:55). If that James really wrote the work that bears his name, then he must have written before A.D. 62 when James suffered martyrdom in Jerusalem. Most scholars, however, regard the work as pseudonymous and point to its cultured Greek language, the address to Jewish Christians outside the land of Israel (the Diaspora), and the debate with a version of Pauline theology. If that is so, an origin in the late first century and in the eastern Mediterranean world seems likely.

Despite its attribution to James "the brother of the Lord," this work had a hard time making its way into the canon of Christian Scripture. And throughout the centuries it has had strong critics, the most notable being Martin Luther who called it the "epistle of straw." The chief problem is its lack of explicit attention to Jesus. The name of Jesus appears only twice in the text—first as part of the letter address (1:1), and then as an introduction to an exhortation ("our glorious Lord Jesus Christ," 2:1). Apart from these two formulaic references, James represents on the surface good Jewish wisdom instruction. Some have called it "sub-Christian."

Surface appearances, however, can be deceiving. When placed in the context of Christian Scripture, James, with its emphasis on the practice of virtue in a community setting and on social justice, makes an important contribution to Christian theology and life. Moreover, there are some links between its sayings and those attributed to Jesus in the Gospels (5:2–5 and Matt 6:19, and 5:12 and Matt 5:34–37), and so James is a witness to the Jesus tradition, if not to Jesus himself. And most important of all is James' attempt at correcting an extreme interpretation of Paul's teachings on faith and works.

In his letters to the Galatians and Romans, Paul insisted that faith (rather than the works of the Jewish Law) is the way by which we come to share in the benefits of Jesus' death and resurrection (justification, reconciliation, salvation, etc.). Paul also insisted that faith naturally expresses itself in good works as the "fruit of the Spirit" (see Gal 5:22–23). So James can hardly be said to attack Paul directly in 2:14–26. Rather, he appears to correct an exaggerated version of Paul's teaching that overemphasized faith and disregarded works. This version of Paul's teaching might suggest that faith makes no moral demands.

In response, James insisted that faith, if not accompanied by good deeds, is dead (2:17), and that faith apart from works is barren (2:20). James goes so far as to enlist the figure of Abraham as support for his position. In Galatians 3 and Romans 4 Paul had pointed to Abraham as one whom God declared righteous (see Gen 15:6) before circumcision and the giving of the Law to Moses. So Paul used Abraham as evidence for his gospel that justification took place through Christ apart from circumcision and the Law. James, however, uses Abraham as evidence for his view that faith apart from works is dead. And so in 2:21–23 James takes the declaration of Abraham's righteousness in Gen 15:6 as a prophecy that was fulfilled by Abraham's willingness to sacrifice his son Isaac in Genesis 22: "Was not our ancestor Abraham justified by works when he offered his son Isaac on the altar?" (2:21)

Social justice is the area in which James makes a most important contribution to Christian thought and action. James defines true religion in a very practical way as "to care for orphans and widows in their distress, and to keep oneself unstained by the world" (1:27). One of James' strong convictions is the reversal of fortunes for rich and poor: The poor will be raised up, and the rich will be brought low (1:9). As a flower withers in the scorching heat, so the rich will wither away "in the midst of a busy life" (1:10–11).

James also insists on no partiality for the rich in the Christian community (2:1–4). If both a rich person and a poor person enter the assembly, they should receive the same treatment. Then in 2:5–7 James shifts from insisting on equality to arguing for the superiority of the poor in God's sight. On the one hand (2:5), God has "chosen the poor in the world to be rich in faith and to be heirs of the kingdom." Here James echoes Jesus' beatitude "Blessed are you poor..." (Luke 6:20) and provides the theological basis for what some call "the preferential option for the poor." Since God prefers the poor, so should those who try to do God's work on earth. On the other hand (2:6–7), the rich make life miserable for the poor by oppressing the poor, dragging them into court, and blaspheming God's name. In 2:8–13 James continues the discussion of partiality for the rich by arguing that it transgresses the commandment to love one's neighbor and other commandments too.

In 5:1–6 James summons the rich to lament over "the miseries that are coming to you." He assumes that the rich are unrighteous and that on the coming day of judgment the rich will have the most to fear. Their "treasure" will be rotting riches, moth-eaten garments, and rusted gold and silver. The grounds for condemning the rich are their withholding the wages of their employees, their living luxuriously while life for the poor is harsh, and their condemning and even murdering the righteous.

There are other memorable teachings in James, especially the instruction about speech and sins of the tongue (3:1–12). And the description of the rite of anointing the sick (5:14–15) and the reference to the value of confessing sins to one another (5:16) have exercised great influence on the sacramental practices of the church. But James is, as we have seen, most famous for its teachings on social justice: no partiality for the rich, God's partiality for the poor, the obligations upon employers to be fair, the condemnation of oppression by the wealthy, and the fleeting character of earthly riches.

James is part of the canon of Christian Scripture. When

read within that collection and in the context of Christian faith, James has important things to say about true religion, faith and works, and social justice. Without its insistence on the practical and communal dimensions of Christian life, the New Testament would lack some essential perspectives.

Questions for Reflection: *Does James really disagree with Paul? What relevance might James have for facing social issues today? Is there a tension between no partiality for the rich and the preferential option for the poor?*

Texts for Special Attention: *James 1:19–27; 3:1–12; and 5:7–11.*

1 Peter

There are many similarities between 1 Peter and Hebrews. Both are sermons or exhortations expressed in the form of a letter. Both assume a social setting in which Christians are a minority ("aliens and exiles" in 1 Pet 2:11, and the wandering people of God in Hebrews). Neither community can offer worldly prestige or power or status. Both communities run the risk of being swallowed up by the larger societies around them. And both writers respond to their community situations by appealing to the person of Jesus—to Christ the Suffering Servant in 1 Peter, and to Christ the high priest in Hebrews.

First Peter is exhortation in letter form. So many are the allusions to baptism that some regard it as originally a baptismal homily. Was it composed by the apostle Peter? That is not impossible, though most scholars regard it as composed in Peter's name (pseudonymous). It appears to have been written in Rome (identified by the code name "Babylon" in 5:13) and addressed to several communities in northern Asia Minor ("Pontus, Galatia, Cappadocia, Asia, and Bithynia," 1:1). If it came directly from Peter, it must have been written in about A.D. 60 (before his martyrdom under the emperor Nero). Some scholars raise the possibility of a Petrine circle at Rome that kept alive the apostle's memory. If it was only written under Peter's name, then a date about A.D. 80 or 90 seems appropriate. As with the secondary Pauline letters, 1 Peter represents what Peter would have said or should have said in the new situation. That situation apparently involved persecution; whether it was political or social is hard to determine.

After the usual letter address (1:1–2), 1 Peter deals with the following topics: Christians as the elect and holy people of God (1:3–2:10), the Christian community as the household of faith (2:11–3:7), suffering as a divine discipline (3:8–4:19), directions for various community members (5:1–11), and final greetings (5:12–14). One of the richest theological documents in the New Testament, 1 Peter gives a glimpse into why early Christians considered Jesus to be so important. It focuses on the significance of Jesus' death and resurrection and is especially appropriate reading for the Easter season and in connection with baptism.

The issues of the person of Jesus (Who is Jesus?) and his significance for Christian life (Why is he important?) cannot be separated in 1 Peter. In fact, 1 Peter is precisely concerned with how these two issues intersect. The letter address (1:1–2) presents a theological formula that sketches the Trinity's role in creating the people of God: "chosen and destined by God the Father, and sanctified by the Spirit, to be obedient to Jesus Christ and to be sprinkled by his blood." Note the double emphasis on Jesus' saving death ("sprinkled by his blood") and his teaching by example ("to be obedient to Jesus Christ").

The first part of 1 Peter (1:3–2:10) is a meditation on how God, through Jesus' death and resurrection, has made the Christian community into an elect and holy people of God. The benediction (1:3–12) celebrates Jesus' resurrection from the dead as the basis of "new birth" and of hope for the future, interprets the present sufferings of Christians as tests or trials to prove the genuineness of their faith, and invokes the Old Testament prophets for confirmation since they foretold "the sufferings destined for Christ and the subsequent glory."

The call to holy living (1:13–25) is based on the holiness of God: "…as he who called you is holy, be holy yourselves in all your conduct" (1:15). Although the present may remain the "time of your exile" (1:17), there is also the firm conviction that Christians have been ransomed "with the precious blood of Christ" (1:19) and "born anew" (1:23).

The meditation ends by identifying Christians in 2:9–10 with terms once applied in Exodus 19 to ancient Israel gathered at Mount Sinai: "…you are a chosen race, a royal priesthood, a holy nation, God's own people." Most of the first readers of 1 Peter were not Jews by birth (see 1:14, 18; 4:3–4). And yet through the power of Jesus' death and resurrection these Gentiles can be reckoned as part of God's chosen people. The mission of the people of God is to "proclaim the mighty acts of him who called you out of darkness into his marvelous light." The role of God's grace in their change of identity from Gentiles to God's people is underlined in the final statement: "Once you were not a people, but now you are God's people; once you had not received mercy, but now you have received mercy."

If 1 Pet 1:3–2:10 is a meditation on the baptismal dignity of Christians, 2:11–3:7 is an instruction on how to live out that dignity in their concrete situation as a religious and social minority in the Roman empire. As such they are "aliens and exiles" (2:11). To change or challenge the prevailing social assumptions was impossible for such a tiny movement.

Therefore they had to accept their social situation and work within it. The ideal is to "conduct yourselves honorably among the Gentiles" (2:12), understanding non-Christians now as the Gentiles. The writer assumes that his readers are involved in their society, and recommends good conduct as a way of impressing non-Christians and leading them to accept and glorify God. The missionary strategy of good example receives its biblical foundation in this passage.

In practice Christians should "accept the authority of every human institution" (2:13) and be exemplary citizens of the Roman empire. Here the advice is reminiscent of Paul's instruction in Romans 13 but very different from what is found in Revelation. Slaves or servants are told in 2:18–25 to defer to their masters; when treated unjustly, they should look to the example of Christ. Wives (3:1–6) should accept the authority of their husbands and dress and act modestly, and husbands (3:7) should show consideration toward their wives. These instructions, of course, echo the household codes in Col 3:18–4:1 and Eph 5:21–6:9. They accept the social and political structures of the Roman empire as realities and seek to lead people to Christian faith by good example and to carve out a place for the church within the world as it was defined for them.

Despite the efforts of early Christians to be "good citizens," they were often the subject of persecution, whether due to the social alienation that resulted from their new way of life (see 4:3–4), or from the political threat that government officials may have perceived them to be. Therefore they needed instruction on how to deal with suffering (3:8–4:19).

The Christian ideal is always to do good and so keep a clear conscience (3:16). But what if one suffers unjustly? Here the advice moves in several directions. First, Christians are not to respond with "evil for evil, or abuse for abuse" (3:9). Instead, they are to repay evil and abuse "with a blessing," thus putting into practice Jesus' teaching about loving enemies. Second, by persisting in good conduct despite the accusations and abuses of others, eventually others will come to see what is really happening and so their detractors will be put to shame (3:16). Third, and most important, there is an appeal to the example of Jesus: "For Christ also suffered for sins once for all, the righteous for the unrighteous, in order to bring you to God" (3:18). Fourth, there is a conviction that "the end of all things is near" (4:7) and that at the last judgment the righteous faithful will be vindicated and the wicked will be punished. Finally, in 4:12–13 there are two interpretations given to the innocent sufferings undergone by Christians: They are a "test" or divine discipline to show the genuineness of their faith, and they are a sharing in Christ's own sufferings. This part of 1 Peter is the most sustained and complete treatment of suffering in the New Testament.

In giving directions for community members (5:1–11), Peter speaks as an elder to other elders and reminds them that all their pastoral activities must be carried out against the horizon of the last judgment when Christ "the chief shepherd appears" (5:4). In the meantime, Christians must regard their present sufferings as temporary: "After you have suffered for a little while, the God of all grace, who has called you to his eternal glory in Christ, will himself restore, support, strengthen, and establish you" (5:10).

First Peter is a theological gem. It offers a marvelous portrait of the role of Jesus' death and resurrection in Christian life. It shows how the gospel can be spread by the exemplary behavior of Christians. And it provides a sustained reflection on suffering and Christian faith. Although it reflects the social assumptions of the past on some issues, 1 Peter can still speak eloquently to all those whose faith makes them "aliens and exiles" in a sinful world.

Questions for Reflection: *What difference do Jesus' death and resurrection make for Christians? How does 1 Peter help Christians to look at and endure their sufferings? Do you see any potential dangers in this advice?*

Texts for Special Attention: *1 Peter 1:13–12; 2:9–10; 4:1–6; and 4:12–19.*

Jude

The letter attributed to Jude is short and polemical. The author identifies himself as "a servant of Jesus Christ and brother of James" (1:1). At this time—the late first century—it may have been considered presumptuous to claim blood relationship with Jesus (see Mark 6:3; Matt 13:55). Rather than developing a portrait of Jesus, the author is satisfied to refer to Jesus in formulaic expressions: "kept safe for Jesus Christ" (1); "our only Master and Lord, Jesus Christ" (4); "our Lord Jesus Christ" (17, 21); and "through Jesus Christ our Lord" (25).

The letter of Jude is both a denunciation and a warning. After the address (1–2), there is a denunciation (3–16) against certain intruders who are seducing good Christians away from "the faith that was once for all entrusted to the saints" (3–4). The opponents are threatened with the kinds of judgments visited upon the unfaithful Israelites of the exodus generation, the fallen angels, and the people of Sodom and Gomorrah (5–7). God will rebuke them as God once rebuked Cain, Balaam, and Korah (11). Since we have only Jude's side of the conversation, it is hard to know what these opponents were teaching and doing. They seem to have been Christians of an unorthodox orientation. They are accused of deviating from the apostolic faith and of committing (probably sexual) immorality. In denouncing them, Jude calls upon examples not only from the Old Testament but also from extrabiblical books in the case of Moses' burial and Enoch's prophecy (14–16).

The warning (17–23) stresses the importance of basing one's life on the apostolic faith described as "the predictions of the apostles" (17) and "your most holy faith" (20). It notes that the apostles foretold that figures such as the present opponents would arise. The positive ideal of Christian life is expressed in a trinitarian formula: "pray in the Holy Spirit; keep yourselves in the love of God; look forward to the mercy of our Lord Jesus Christ that leads to eternal life" (21).

The concluding benediction (24–25) asks that God may keep the recipients from falling into the traps set by the opponents so that they may be able to greet the last judgment as the occasion of their vindication and lasting joy.

The letter of Jude is important for its emphasis on the apostolic faith as a firm and objective foundation for Christian life. It insists that Christian faith and Christian life form a single entity. It accuses the opponents (who regarded themselves as Christians) of bad faith and of a wicked way of life.

The problem posed by the letter of Jude is that we do not hear the other side. We do not really know what the opponents were teaching and doing. In fact, we do not really know how the author himself defined the content of the apostolic faith that he regarded as so important. His frequent use of credal formulas in referring to Jesus suggests that he understood the apostolic faith to be an objective body of truths that had been transmitted to the church. But which truths were they? The letter assumes a sharp division between orthodoxy and heresy. But it does not help us 1900 years later to grasp how they are to be defined.

Questions for Reflection: *How do you define the apostolic faith? What belongs to it?*

Texts for Special Attention: *Jude 3–4 and 17–23.*

2 Peter

Attributed to the apostle Peter, 2 Peter is generally regarded as a late first or early second century revision and expansion of the letter of Jude. Both writers were convinced that the apostolic faith was the best defense against error and immorality. Most of Jude is incorporated into 2 Peter. The author of 2 Peter, however, softens the denunciatory tone of Jude by including examples of God's mercy. He also corrects Jude's order of biblical examples and omits the references to books outside the Old Testament. The most significant issue addressed in 2 Peter is the apparent delay of the second coming of Christ.

Following the address (1:1–2), Peter reflects on the vocation of the Christian (1:3–11) and on his own status as an apostle (1:12–21), denounces his opponents in terms largely taken over from Jude (2:1–22), deals with the opponents' skepticism about the second coming of Christ (3:1–13), and provides a final exhortation and doxology (3:14–18).

The theological significance of 2 Peter resides primarily in its treatment of the second coming of Christ. The opponents are identified as the "scoffers" who will come in the last days (2 Pet 3:3; Jude 14–16). Their scoffing concerns the apparent delay of Christ's second coming: "Where is the promise of his coming? For ever since our ancestors died, all things continue as they were from the beginning of creation" (3:4). Thus they hold up to mockery the failure of the new heaven and new earth to materialize.

In response to this challenge, the author of 2 Peter in 3:5–10 makes four arguments. First, in 3:5–7 he challenges their assumption that the world is always the same. Rather, the earth was created by God, underwent destruction by the flood in Noah's time, and will be destroyed again by fire (the only New Testament evidence for this idea). Second, in 3:8 he appeals to Psalm 90:4 ("for a thousand years in your sight are like yesterday") to suggest that human standards of calculation are not applicable in measuring God's activity. Third, he suggests that the delay of Christ's second coming is due to God's mercy and patience in order to give as many people as possible the opportunity to repent before the last judgment. Finally, in 3:10 he uses the motif of Christ coming like a thief to indicate that the second coming will be sudden and unexpected. The implication is that one should always be on guard, since the second coming might happen at any time.

As in Jude, so in 2 Peter there is a strong emphasis on the apostolic faith. Here the appeals to the apostolic credentials of Peter are even stronger. Peter assures the readers that they have received "a faith as precious as ours" (1:1). That faith consists not in "cleverly designed myths" (1:16) but in direct experience of the person of Jesus. In the context of a challenge to belief in Christ's second coming, Peter puts forward his eyewitness experience of the transfiguration of Jesus (1:17–18; see Mark 9:2–8). The transfiguration, as an anticipation of the full glory of the risen Christ, is taken as an anticipatory confirmation that Christ will indeed come again. By placing the apostles alongside the holy prophets (3:2) the author makes them a venerated group who have mediated Christ's teachings to the church. Since the opponents seem to be twisting Paul's teaching about freedom for their own ends (see 2:19), he feels obliged to show that Paul's teaching is the same as his own.

The author's comment on Paul's letters indicates that even in antiquity they were controversial: "There are some things in them hard to understand, which the ignorant and unstable twist to their own destruction, as they do the other scriptures" (3:16). Peter claims to be an authoritative interpreter not only of Paul's letters but also of the Old Testament Scriptures. Because the prophets were "moved by the Holy Spirit" (1:21), no prophecy of Scripture is a matter of one's own interpretation. The correct interpretation is the one intended by the Holy Spirit who is now understood to speak through the apostles.

The author of 2 Peter takes a stricter attitude toward Scripture than Jude does. Thus in chapter 2 he excises several legendary and nonbiblical features from Jude: the angels' descent from heaven, the idea of Michael and Satan fighting over Moses' body, and the quotation from 1 Enoch. In 2:4–8 he rearranges the Old Testament incidents in their proper biblical order: the angels' sin, the flood, and the destruction of Sodom and Gomorrah. He also balances the negative episodes by the positive examples of Noah and Lot.

Second Peter is presented as the testament of Peter; that is, his words of advice shortly before his death ("since I know that my death will come soon," 1:14). The author took over most of the denunciation from Jude and expanded it in chapter 2. He also presents some positive teachings on Christian life. According to 1:3, "God has given us everything needed for life and goodness." This text makes God the source of all Christian virtues. The foundational virtue is faith, which animates and works with the other virtues: goodness, knowledge, self-control, endurance, godliness, mutual affection, and love. The practice of Christian virtue is not self-generated, nor is it a personal achievement for which one can take credit. Rather, the practice of Christian virtue is a way of responding to God's grace or favor and of showing forth the glory of God.

Many scholars regard 2 Peter as the latest document in the New Testament. This is so chiefly because of the issues it treats and the way it deals with them: the delay of Christ's second coming, the content and interpretation of Scripture, the emphasis on the apostolic faith, and the approach to Christian life. As such, 2 Peter is a bridge to the early patristic writings and the shape of Christian faith from the second century onward.

Questions for Reflection: *How would you answer the opponents' objection in 2 Peter 3:4 about the delay of the parousia? How does the transfiguration function in Peter's argument? Where do human virtues fit in Christian life?*

Texts for Special Attention: *2 Peter 1:3–11 and 3:5–10.*

King of Kings, Lord of Lords: Revelation

Whenever I teach a course or do a workshop on the book of Revelation, I ask the participants why they chose to study this book. There are two recurrent answers. The first is, "I have tried to read this book many times but I can never get far in understanding it." The second is, "Someone I know and love is deeply 'into' this book, and I need to understand it to understand them better." Revelation is a difficult book. It also exercises strong influence in certain circles. Rather than avoiding the book or fearing it, we should try to appreciate its distinctive contributions to our understanding of Jesus and Christian life.

Revelation is especially important because of its vision of

the risen Christ and its encouragement for Christians facing persecution. The author was a Jewish-Christian prophet named John (most likely neither the apostle nor the evangelist). He was in exile on the island of Patmos (1:9) for his witness to Christ. He was granted a visionary experience of the risen Christ on "the Lord's day" (1:10) and sought to share it with members of seven Christian communities in western Asia Minor (present-day Turkey). The book's composition is usually placed late (A.D. 95–96) in the emperor Domitian's reign, though it may contain material from Nero's time.

The communities addressed in Revelation were facing persecution for their Christian faith. This persecution was probably a limited program promoted by a local political and/or religious official. It focused on worshipping the emperor as a god and the goddess Roma as the personification of the empire. The Christians of western Asia Minor had to confront the question, Who really is Lord and God? Their answer—Jesus and his heavenly Father—would make participation in these civil cults impossible on the grounds of conscience.

The book of Revelation is an apocalypse or revelation (1:1) and a prophecy (1:3) in letter form (1:4). It is written in a Semitic Greek style (of poor quality) and is full of allusions to the Old Testament (which the writer knew very well indeed). It features various series of "sevens"—letters (2:1–3:22), seals (6:1–8:1), trumpets (8:7–11:19), bowls (16:1–21), and end-time events (19:11–22:5). The book need not be read as a detailed forecast of future events or as a historical curiosity. Rather, it can and does speak to us today, especially with regard to its fundamental question, Who is Lord and God?

The Risen Christ and the Seven Churches (1–3)

John's book is a revelation of (from and about) Jesus Christ. In the prologue (1:1–3) John the seer traces the revelation that he received to an angel, through Christ, and back to God. The revelation concerns "what must soon take place." Those who read and those who hear it and act upon it are declared blessed or happy.

The address (1:4–8) begins according to the convention of letters in antiquity: "John to the seven churches that are in Asia." But John goes on to describe Jesus the risen Lord in terms that would have been especially meaningful for Christians facing persecution: "…the faithful witness, the firstborn of the dead, and the ruler of the kings of the earth" (1:5). As the risen one, Jesus is the model for suffering Christians and the ground of their hope in God's power to save and vindicate them. Likewise, the death of Jesus ("by his blood") is understood to be a proof of God's love and the basis of Christian freedom (1:5–6). Through Jesus' death and resurrection, God has made them a "kingdom" and "priests"—members of God's kingdom now and totally devoted to the worship of God (see Exod 19:6; Isa 61:6; 1 Pet 2:5, 9). The effects of Jesus' saving death and resurrection are in turn based in the omnipotent Lord God "who is and who was and who is to come."

The inaugural vision of the risen Christ (1:9–20) is foundational for the letters that follow immediately, and indeed for the whole book. In exile on Patmos for bearing witness to Jesus, John first hears a voice telling him to write what he sees to the seven churches (1:9–11). Next he recounts in 1:12–16 what he saw: a glorious figure who can be described only with the help of images taken mainly from the Old Testament. Then he tells what he heard: the voice of the glorious figure who identifies himself as the risen Christ. The glorious Christ affirms that he is "the first and the last, and the living one. I was dead, and see I am alive forever and ever" (1:17–18). By his death and resurrection Christ has conquered death. His resurrection is the ground of hope for us all. His victory is the pledge and guarantee of God's victory over those persons and forces who are hostile to God's people.

The seven churches addressed in chapters 2–3 were in western Asia Minor (present-day Turkey): Ephesus (2:1–7), Smyrna (2:8–11), Pergamum (2:12–17), Thyatira (2:18–29),

Sardis (3:1–6), Philadelphia (3:7–13), and Laodicea (3:14–21). The messages to them are from the risen Lord. The messages are pastoral reports on the state of each church and warnings to reform where necessary. Each letter follows the same outline: a command from the risen Christ to John to write to the "angel" of the church (its guardian angel or perhaps its bishop), the identification of the speaker as the risen Christ with reference to images from the inaugural vision, praise and/or blame regarding the state of the community, a call to pay attention, and a promise to those who remain faithful that they will share eternal life with Christ.

Several communities are praised for their ability to recognize and resist false teachers, for their patient endurance in persecution, and for their fidelity to Christ even to the point of death. But there are also serious problems. Some communities have lost their religious fervor; they are judged to have "abandoned the love you had at first" (2:4) or to be spiritually "dead" (3:1) or "lukewarm" (3:16). Some are being led astray by teachers who would allow Christians to participate in the cult of the emperor and the goddess Roma (2:14, 20). Such teachers are given the biblical names of Balaam and Jezebel, who tried to lead ancient Israel away from the worship of Yahweh.

There are also pressures from local Jewish communities (2:9; 3:9) that wanted to keep themselves separate from what was still largely a Jewish Christian movement and so avoid jeopardizing their privileged status within the Roman empire as a legally recognized religious group (*religio licita*). And most importantly, there is the expectation from local Roman officials and the general public that Christians should join in what they regarded as part of the civil religion of the Roman empire. This included honoring the emperor as a god and honoring Roma as the personification of the empire.

To those who overcome these obstacles the risen Christ promises eternal happiness with God. Various images are used: eating from the tree of life (2:7), avoiding the second death (2:11), being given the "hidden manna" and the "white stone" (2:17), being granted a share in the Messiah's authority (2:27–28), wearing white garments and having a place in the book of life (3:5), being a pillar in God's temple (3:12), and having a place with Christ at God's throne (3:21).

Questions for Reflection: *How is the risen Jesus described? Why is the risen Jesus a source of hope for suffering Christians? Do you see parallels between the churches addressed in chapters 2–3 and the churches today?*

Texts for Special Attention: *Revelation 1:12–20 and 3:14–21.*

The Slain Lamb and God's Justice (4–11)

The Jesus of Revelation is the risen Jesus whom God has exalted to eternal glory. In chapters 4 and 5, John is granted an experience of his glory. He sees an "open door" in heaven and is summoned by a voice, "Come up here, and I will show you what must take place after this" (4:1). What John sees is the heavenly court, a throne room that far surpassed that of any earthly king or emperor. It is the throne of God. This throne is surrounded by twenty-four elders and four living creatures (see Ezek 1:10). The visual splendor of the scene is enhanced by the songs of the heavenly chorus: "Holy, holy, holy, the Lord God Almighty..." and "You are worthy, our Lord and God, to receive glory and honor and power..." (4:8, 11). The scene emphasizes the power of God as creator and sustainer of all things. No human emperor can compare with this Lord.

The risen Jesus is introduced into the vision of the heavenly court by the search for someone worthy to open the scroll with seven seals (5:1–5). Just as John is about to despair because apparently no one can be found worthy, one of the elders assures him that "the Lion of the tribe of Judah" (see Gen 49:9) and "the Root of David" (see Isa 11:1, 10) is indeed worthy.

These titles refer to the messianic heritage of Jesus. At last, John sees the risen Jesus—paradoxically as the Slain Lamb (5:6–7). Jesus is now a glorious figure and yet bears the marks of his death. This image respects both his death and resurrection, which are viewed here as elsewhere in the New Testament as two aspects of one event. Since his death and resurrection have inaugurated the series of end-time events, it is appropriate that he should open the seven seals and reveal what is written in the scroll.

The appearance of the Slain Lamb is accompanied by three cycles of praise from the heavenly chorus (5:8–14). The song of the four living creatures and the twenty-four elders focuses on the redemptive power of Jesus' death ("for you were slaughtered and by your blood you ransomed for God saints…") and its consequences ("you have made them to be a kingdom and priests," see 1:6). The heavenly hosts acclaim the Slain Lamb worthy to receive "power and wealth and wisdom and might and honor and glory and blessing." Then all creation ascribes blessing and honor and glory and might "to the one seated on the throne and to the Lamb."

Jesus the Slain Lamb and glorious risen Christ surpasses in dignity all creatures in heaven or on earth. Born into Israel's royal line, he deserves the praise normally reserved for God ("the one seated on the throne"). His death and resurrection are assigned a sacrificial significance (the Slain Lamb) and a redemptive significance ("by your blood you ransomed"). The risen Jesus alone is qualified to open the seven seals and initiate the series of end-time events.

These events are to begin with the opening of the seven seals (6:1–8:1) and the sounding of the seven trumpets (8:2–11:19). Each member in the two series is accompanied by some disaster or punishment visited upon the earth. So the opening of the seven seals brings war, strife among nations, famine, death, persecution, and the "great tribulation." Then after an interlude (7:1–17), there is with the opening of the seventh seal "silence in heaven for about half an hour" (8:1). Likewise, the sounding of the seven trumpets brings hail and fire, the seas becoming blood, bitter waters, darkness, locusts, and a fierce army from the East. Many of these events recall the ten plagues visited upon Egypt in Moses' time (see Exodus 7–12). Then after another interlude (10:1–11:14), there is with the sounding of the seventh trumpet a chorus of praise celebrating the real ruler of the world: "The kingdom of the world has become the kingdom of our Lord, and of his Messiah, and he will reign forever and ever" (11:15). Are the first two series of sevens independent and self-contained? Or is there a linear progress? That remains a problem throughout the book, which gives some indications of a straight-line development and other indications that the same things are being repeated with slightly different images.

The goal of these disasters seems to be to encourage

sinful humankind to repent. But "they did not repent" (9:20–21). What is bad news for sinners, however, is good news for those who remain faithful to God and the Slain Lamb. In the interlude in 7:1–17 the 144,000 representatives of the people of God emerge victorious from the great tribulation: "They have washed their robes and made them white in the blood of the Lamb" (7:14). In the interlude in 11:3–14 the "two witnesses," who recall the figures of Moses and Elijah, though put to death, are raised from the dead and invited to "come up here"—to heaven to be with God and the Lamb. In both scenes God remains faithful to those who remain faithful to God (even to the point of death). They will share the life and glory of the risen Jesus.

What is at stake in the seven seals and the seven trumpets is the justice of God. Beneath the spectacular images and loud voices is the conviction that God must ultimately punish the wicked and reward the righteous. The law of retribution holds, but its definitive execution is in the future. If not now, when? Since in the present the righteous are suffering and the wicked appear to be triumphing, then the ultimate vindication of the former and the punishment of the wicked must take place in God's own future.

Questions for Reflection: *How are Jesus' death and resurrection interpreted in this section? What is the point of describ-*

ing Jesus as the Slain Lamb? How is God's justice upheld, and what does this mean for Christian life in the present?

Texts for Special Attention: *Revelation 4:1–5:14.*

The Unholy Trinity and the Seven Bowls (12–16)

The central portion of the book—chapters 12 to 14—deals with God's definitive victory over evil embodied in an "unholy trinity" and with the present sufferings of God's people on earth (the church). The chief figure in the unholy trinity is Satan, who is variously known as the great dragon, the ancient serpent, the Devil, and the deceiver of the whole world (12:9). Because Satan has been defeated in heaven (chapter 12), he vents his anger against the church through the Beast from the Sea (the Roman emperor) and the Beast from the Earth (the local official responsible for promoting the emperor cult and the persecution of the Christians). In the end (chapter 14) the companions of the Lamb will be kept safe, and at the final judgment the wicked will be punished and the righteous will be vindicated.

The woman "clothed with the sun" (12:1) is the mother

of the Messiah. She is Israel, the people of God, and by extension the church and Mary the mother of Jesus. As she is about to give birth, the great red dragon (Satan) seeks to devour her son but fails to do so. That her son is the Messiah is indicated by the expression "one who is to rule all the nations with a rod of iron" (12:5 = Ps 2:9, which is a messianic psalm). The focus here is entirely on Jesus' birth and his being taken up "to God and to his throne" (12:5), which is a way of talking about Jesus' death, resurrection, ascension, and exaltation taken as a single event.

The exaltation of Jesus the Messiah marks the decisive defeat of Satan and his expulsion from the heavenly court (12:7–9). Having been thrown down to earth, Satan can cause trouble for God's people on earth but only for a short time (12:12). Even so, God provides protection for the woman (the church) and her offspring (the faithful Christians). While Satan no longer has real power against God and the Lamb, he can still stir up persecution against those "who keep the commandments of God and hold the testimony of Jesus" (12:17). The various scenes in Revelation 12 explain how Jesus in his birth and exaltation has defeated the Evil One in heaven and how at the same time the Christians on earth still suffer persecutions (because Satan is behind them).

The agents of this particular persecution are the Roman emperor who is the Beast from the Sea (13:1–10) and the local official who is the Beast from the Earth (13:11–18). Described in terms from Daniel 7, the emperor is the object of worship and speaks "blasphemous words" by demanding to be called "Lord" and "God." The local official seems to be promoting the emperor cult by spectacular shows and forcing his subjects to display marks of loyalty toward the emperor (the mark of the Beast, 13:16–17). The number of the Beast/emperor is 666. This number most likely corresponds to the numerical value of the name of the emperor Nero (the archetype for evil emperors, especially Domitian) when the name Nero(n) Caesar is written in Hebrew characters where the letters stand for numbers: NRWN QSR = 50 + 200 + 6 + 50 + 100 + 60 + 200 = 666.

Who really is Lord and God? This is the central issue of the book of Revelation. The answer for John and the Christians is that the true Lord and God is the Slain Lamb and the One who sits on the throne. In 14:1–5 there is a vision of the Slain Lamb and his 144,000 companions who have been "redeemed from humankind." They are further identified as those "who have not defiled themselves with women, for they are virgins" (14:4). This description most likely refers not to celibacy but rather to the Christians who refused to participate in worship of the emperor. In the background is the biblical idea (see especially Hosea) that idolatry is adultery or fornication.

The unholy trinity and their devotees must eventually face the judgment of God and Jesus the Son of Man (14:6–20). A series of angelic proclamations in 14:6–13 announces that

Babylon the great (surely a name for Rome) is fallen, and that those who have worshiped the beast and bear his mark deserve fierce punishments. Two judgment scenes—the harvest of the Son of Man (14:14–16; see Joel 3:12–13), and the divine warrior treading the winepress (14:17–20; see Isa 63:1–6)—reinforce the idea of God's swift and decisive judgment upon those who persecute God's people and upon the unholy trinity that is ultimately responsible for the persecution.

The various episodes in Revelation 12–14 explain who Jesus is: the Messiah of Israel, the exalted one, the one who broke Satan's power, and the one who will condemn the enemies of God's people and vindicate the faithful witnesses. They also explain Jesus' significance for suffering Christians: He is their leader in the present as well as the ground of their hope for the future.

The last seven plagues (or bowls) in Revelation 15–16 take the form of the seven bowls of God's anger poured out upon the earth. The victory song that introduces them (15:3–4) stresses the omnipotence of God ("Lord God the almighty") and the justice of God ("just and true are your ways…your just judgments have been revealed"). The series of seven bowls echoes the ten plagues visited upon Egypt in Moses' time (see Exodus 7–12 and Revelation 8–9). They bring evil sores or ulcers, turn the waters into blood, darken the earth, and so forth. The targets of these plagues are those "who had the mark of the beast and who worshiped its image" (16:2). Again the goal of their repentance has not been attained (16:9, 11). And again the justice of God is celebrated: "Yes, O Lord God the Almighty, your judgments are true and just!" (16:7). The seventh bowl is directed at "the great Babylon" (16:19), thus preparing for the judgment scenes against Rome in chapters 17 and 18.

Questions for Reflection: *What aspects of Jesus and of God are emphasized in these scenes? How are evil and innocent suffering explained? How might these scenes encourage suffering Christians?*

Texts for Special Attention: *Revelation 12:1–17 and 14:1–5.*

The Two Cities (17–22)

The final chapters of Revelation feature a sharp contrast between Rome and the New Jerusalem. In chapter 17 the goddess Roma and the emperor—the objects of worship according to the religious program of the local official in western Asia Minor—are parodied in 17:1–6 as a prostitute and a beast, respectively. Lest anyone miss the point, John states: "The woman you saw is the great city that rules over the kings of the earth" (17:18).

The fall of Rome is accompanied by proclamations from angels (18:1–8, 21–24) and laments from kings, merchants, and sailors (18:9–19). Of course, Rome had not yet fallen when John wrote Revelation. But in light of John's identification of Rome with biblical Babylon and his conviction that through Jesus' death and resurrection Satan's power had been broken, Rome was as good as already fallen. The charge against Rome is that it seduced the nations within its empire to idolatry and immoral behavior (18:3, 9). Those who did business with Rome stand back in amazement at the suddenness and completeness of her fall.

A peculiar feature in Revelation 18 is the angel's summons: "Render to her as she herself has rendered, and repay her double for her deeds" (18:6). The command seems to be directed to the Christians (as in 18:4, "Come out of her, my people"). If so, this would be the only deviation in Revelation from a stance of nonviolent resistance to Rome. Everywhere else, it is understood that God, Christ, and the angels will punish the enemies of God's people on earth. Perhaps then the summons is directed to angels.

The defeat of Rome will be the victory for God's faithful people: "God has given judgment for you against her" (18:20).

The victory is celebrated by four Alleluias and a beatitude (19:1–10). The chorus proclaims the justice of God: "he has judged the great whore who corrupted the earth with her fornication, and he has avenged the blood of his servants" (19:2). It also proclaims the marriage feast of the Lamb (the risen Christ) and the bride (the church): "…the marriage of the Lamb has come, and his bride has made herself ready" (19:7). The simplicity and purity of the Lamb's bride (the church) contrasts with the garish dress (17:4–5) and immoral behavior (18:3) of the prostitute (Roma). The truly "blessed" ones (19:9) are those (the faithful Christians) who are invited to the marriage supper of the Lamb. Despite appearances in the present, their fidelity must be rewarded just as Rome must fall.

The contrast between the two cities is interrupted by the final series of seven end-time events: the appearance of Christ the warrior (19:11–16), his victory in battle (19:17–21), the binding of Satan for a thousand years (20:1–3), the first resurrection for the martyrs (20:4–6), the final defeat of Satan (20:7–10), the last judgment (20:11–15), and the new heaven and the new earth (21:1–8).

In the first scene the risen Christ appears as a warrior seated on a white horse. He is called "the Word of God" (19:13) and the "King of kings and Lord of lords" (19:16). As such, the risen Christ is far superior to any human ruler, including the Roman emperor. In the battle he proves himself to be the victor (see 19:20) over "the beast" (the emperor) and "the false prophet" (the local official), and he makes possible the binding of Satan for a thousand years (20:2–3). The defeat of this "unholy trinity" is at the same time the vindication of those witnesses to Christ who have been faithful unto death. Just as God vindicated Jesus in his resurrection, so the martyrs will come to life and reign with Christ for a thousand years (20:4). This in turn sets the stage for the final defeat of Satan and his eternal punishment with the beast and the false prophet (20:10), as well as the last judgment of all the dead. These climactic scenes introduce the other city: "the holy city, the New Jerusalem, coming down out of heaven from God" (21:2).

The New Jerusalem originates with God and reflects the glory of God (21:10–11). Whereas the symbol of Rome was a prostitute, the symbol of the New Jerusalem is "the bride, the wife of the Lamb" (21:9). Its high walls, gates, and size surpass the size and splendor of any human city, including Rome. Its most peculiar feature is the absence of a temple (21:22). Since God and the Lamb are in the New Jerusalem, there is no need for a temple. Whereas Babylon/Rome was full of abominations (17:4), nothing unclean or abominable is present in the New Jerusalem (21:27). Those who live in this city have the Lord God as their light and reign forever (22:5).

The book ends (22:6–21) with a collection of ten sayings that concern the authenticity of the prophet's message, the imminence of Christ's coming, and the need for the readers to remain faithful to the one who is "the Alpha and the Omega" (22:13; see 1:8 where this title applies to God) and "the bright morning star" (22:16, an allusion to Christ's resurrection as the first in a series). The hope and longing expressed throughout the book burst out with a final prayer in 22:20: "Come, Lord Jesus!"

Revelation is a difficult book. It addressed a concrete situation long ago and far away, with images and symbols that sometimes defy comprehension. It so emphasizes the justice of God that little room is left for the mercy of God (except to faithful Christians). It shows no interest in the life and teachings of the earthly Jesus. Its focus is the risen Christ and the consequences of his death and resurrection.

The Jesus of Revelation is the glorious risen Christ who appears to John (1:12–20), the Slain Lamb worthy to open the seven seals (5:6–14), and the Divine Warrior who defeats the "unholy trinity" (19:11–21). He is King of kings and Lord of lords.

The Jesus of Revelation cannot be understood apart from the life-situation of the Christians to whom the book was originally addressed. They were facing a crisis of conscience. Could they participate in worship of the emperor and the goddess Roma? John's answer was "No!" Adherence to his uncompromising stance could and did lead to suffering and even martyrdom.

While reading the book with reference to its original circumstances is essential, the problem of suffering for witness to the gospel has affected and still affects many Christians. John deals with the problem by appealing to what has already happened through Jesus' death and resurrection (the preliminary defeat of the evil powers, and the redemption of those who believe in Jesus) and to what the almighty and just God will surely do in the future through the King of kings (the complete and final defeat of evil, and the fullness of God's kingdom).

Revelation is a book of songs that celebrate the risen Christ and the justice of God. For Christians, especially those living under pressure and facing hard decisions, it continues to offer hope, encouragement, and joy.

Questions for Reflection: *In what sense is the risen Christ "King of kings and Lord of lords?" How do you respond to the portrayal of Christ as the Divine Warrior? What is the place of God's justice in the fate of the two cities?*

Texts for Special Attention: *Revelation 19:11–16 and 21:22–22:5.*

For Further Study

Achtemeier, P. J. *1 Peter.* Minneapolis: Fortress, 1996.

Ashton, J. *Understanding the Fourth Gospel.* Oxford, New York: Oxford University Press, 1992.

Attridge, H. W. *The Epistle to the Hebrews.* Philadelphia: Fortress, 1988.

Brown, R. E. *The Gospel According to John.* Garden City, New York: Doubleday, 1966, 1970.

———. *An Introduction to New Testament Christology,* New York: Paulist, 1994.

———. *An Introduction to the New Testament.* New York: Doubleday, 1997.

Byrne, B. *Romans.* Collegeville, Minnesota: Liturgical Press, 1996.

Dunn, J. D. G. *The Epistles to the Colossians and Philemon.* Grand Rapids, Michigan: Eerdmans, 1996.

———. *The Theology of Paul the Apostle.* Grand Rapids, Michigan: Eerdmans, 1997.

Fitzmyer, J. A. *The Gospel According to Luke.* Garden City, New York: Doubleday, 1981, 1985.

———. *Romans.* New York: Doubleday, 1993.

Harrington, D. J. *The Gospel of Matthew.* Collegeville, Minnesota: Liturgical Press, 1991.

———. *Interpreting the New Testament.* Collegeville, Minnesota: Liturgical Press, 1988.

Harrington, W. J. *Revelation.* Collegeville, Minnesota: Liturgical Press, 1993.

Hays, R. B. *The Moral Vision of the New Testament.* San Francisco: Harper, 1996.

Hooker, M. D. *The Gospel According to Saint Mark.* Peabody, Massachusetts: Hendrickson, 1993.

Johnson, L. T. *The Acts of the Apostles.* Collegeville, Minnesota: Liturgical Press, 1992.

———. *The Gospel of Luke.* Collegeville, Minnesota: Liturgical Press, 1991.

———. *The Letter of James.* New York: Doubleday, 1995.

Karris, R. J. and D. Bergant (eds.). *Collegeville Bible Commentary.* Collegeville, Minnesota: Liturgical Press, 1989.

Matera, F. J. *Galatians.* Collegeville, Minnesota: Liturgical Press, 1992.

Meeks, W. A. *The First Urban Christians.* New Haven, Connecticut: Yale University Press, 1983.

Meier, J. P. *A Marginal Jew: Rethinking the Historical Jesus.* New York: Doubleday, 1991, 1994.

Moloney, F. J. *The Gospel of John.* Collegeville, Minnesota: Liturgical Press, 1998.

Murphy, R. A., J. A. Fitzmyer, and R. E. Brown (eds.), *The New Jerome Biblical Commentary.* Englewood Cliffs, New Jersey: Prentice-Hall, 1990.

Richard, E. *First and Second Thessalonians.* Collegeville, Minnesota: Liturgical Press, 1995.

Schnackenburg, R. *The Johannine Epistles.* New York: Crossroad, 1992.

Stuhlmueller, C. (ed.). *The Collegeville Pastoral Dictionary of Biblical Theology.* Collegeville, Minnesota: Liturgical Press, 1996.

Wright, N. T. *Jesus and the Victory of God.* Minneapolis: Fortress, 1996.

Young, F. *The Theology of the Pastoral Letters.* Cambridge, New York: Cambridge University Press, 1994.

Index

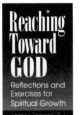